Faulkner, Modernism, and Film:
Faulkner and Yoknapatawpha,
1978

# Faulkner, Modernism, and Film:

FAULKNER AND YOKNAPATAWPHA,
1978

EDITED BY
EVANS HARRINGTON
AND
ANN J. ABADIE

UNIVERSITY PRESS OF MISSISSIPPI
JACKSON • 1979

*This volume is authorized & sponsored by the
University of Mississippi*

*Library of Congress Cataloging in Publication Data*

Faulkner and Yoknapatawpha Conference, 5th, University of Mississippi, 1978.
    Faulkner, modernism, and film.

    1. Faulkner, William, 1897–1962—Congresses.
I. Harrington, Evans.  II. Abadie, Ann J.  III. Title.
PS3511.A86Z489 1978      813'.5'2      79-11298
ISBN 0–87805–102–3
ISBN 0–87805–103–1 pbk.

IN MEMORY OF
WILL GEER
1902–1978

# Contents

# Contents

# Introduction

Malcolm Cowley, guest lecturer for the University of Mississippi's first Faulkner and Yoknapatawpha Conference in 1974, returned to William Faulkner's hometown to speak at the fifth of these annual conferences that have been attended by persons from every state in the U.S. and from several foreign countries. Quite appropriately, Cowley opened the 1978 meeting by asking why Faulkner's work has elicited an overwhelming response from a devoted body of readers and scholars. Since the Mississippi writer has attracted readers from around the world and has in recent years received more critical and scholarly attention than any other American writer, with thousands of articles and more than two hundred books devoted entirely to his fiction, Cowley's question is a challenging one. Faulkner himself probably could not have answered it, for in 1953 he wrote, in a letter to his friend Joan Williams, "And now I realize . . . what an amazing gift I had: uneducated in every formal sense, without even very literate, let alone literary, companions, yet to have made the things I made. I dont know where it came from." One answer, though, is given in Cowley's "Magic in Faulkner," printed here as the first of eleven essays originally presented as lectures at the Faulkner and Yoknapatawpha Conference held on the Oxford campus of the University of Mississippi on July 30 through August 4, 1978.

Commenting on the magical or mythopoeic side of Faulkner's work, Cowley explains one major source of Faulkner's powerful effect on his readers—his ability to use the rich resources of his unconscious in the creation of mythical characters and stories with universal correspondences. Cowley attributes the weakness of *A Fable* to its being *"willed* as a parable," unlike the great novels written between 1929 and 1943 for which Faulkner "dipped into his unconscious memories as into a barrel, confident that he would find there all the moving stories since the beginning of time." Faulkner's great novels, according to Cowley, embody a number of myths or legends, all relating to the South but with each one treating different aspects of southern society. Although his observations have application to all of Faulkner's works, Cowley concentrates on "The Bear" from *Go Down, Moses*. He describes this story as the most obvious example of Faulkner's power to create myths that correspond to patterns preexisting in the human unconscious and that therefore appeal to feelings buried deep in the minds of readers.

Cowley emphasizes the rituals of nature in Faulkner's great legend of the Mississippi wilderness. Thomas Daniel Young in his essay on *The Unvanquished* is also concerned with rituals, but with those of southern society. Just as lumbermen destroyed the wilderness, the Civil War destroyed the social order that existed in the antebellum South. This destructive process, which Faulkner shows through his characters Rosa Millard, John Sartoris, and Drusilla Hawks, is carefully analyzed in Young's "Pioneering on Principle, or How a Traditional Society May Be Dissolved." Another southern legend, that of Thomas Sutpen and his family, is discussed in Young's second essay, "Narration as Creative Act: The Role of Quentin Compson in *Absalom, Absalom!*"

Other aspects of Faulkner's literary art are considered in the essays of Hugh Kenner and Ilse Dusoir Lind. In "Faulkner and Joyce," Kenner compares *Ulysses* and *The Sound and the Fury*,

concluding that from Joyce Faulkner learned narrative techniques and inherited an ideal reader, one "who will gather and
store up transient expressive satisfactions . . . and even read the
book several times." Also, Kenner points out that Faulkner very
early perceived the chronicle of an entire Irish family revealed
in what is superficially the story of one day in the life of Stephen Dedalus. Long before critics and scholars recognized
these "Dublin devices," Faulkner used them "for Mississippi
novels equally exact in their genealogies, chronologies, viewpoints, time schemes." In his second essay, "Faulkner and the
Avant-Garde," Kenner also considers Joyce and other creators
of international modernism whose innovative techniques made
possible the peculiar sort of intensely local literature Faulkner
wrote. Although not a member of this avant-garde group of cosmopolitan writers, Faulkner used their expressive devices, graft-
ing modernist innovations to works rooted in the ancient tradition of oral storytelling. Kenner's complex and brilliant essay
helps us understand why readers of Faulkner's Yoknapatawpha
fiction are required to know as much about the people and
places and history of Lafayette County, Mississippi, as its own
residents know. It also helps us understand why Faulkner's
achievements were not first recognized in his hometown, but in
such places as New York and Paris.

British and European influences on Faulkner's work are also
surveyed in Ilse Dusoir Lind's essays, but her concern is with
his responsiveness to the visual and theatrical arts. In "The Effect of Painting on Faulkner's Poetic Form," Lind discusses the
writer's early drawing and painting and shows how his artistic
apprenticeship and his visits to art galleries during his 1925
trip to Europe served him in his writing. Lind attributes Faulkner's extensive use of light and color to his admiration of such
painters as Rembrandt, Gauguin, Degas, and Cézanne. She also
suggests some specific paintings that Faulkner described in
meaningful ways in his fiction. Turning to the theatrical arts for

Introduction

her second essay, "Faulkner's Uses of Poetic Drama," Lind lists
a wide variety of professional and student productions that
were presented at the University of Mississippi between 1907
and 1920. During this time, at what was then an isolated university in the backwoods of Mississippi, the young Faulkner
could have seen many of the world's great dramas, presented
mainly because of the influence of dedicated and talented faculty members. One of these was Stark Young, who later became
a major American drama critic; another was Calvin S. Brown,
who studied classical drama in Greece and later edited a collection of British drama. Lind then looks at Faulkner's own
play, *The Marionettes*, and discusses the influence of the drama
on his fiction. She notes, for instance, that *Light in August* has
numerous theatrical analogies and at least one reference to another art form, film. In pointing out that Faulkner describes
Joe Christmas's horseback ride as having "a strange, dreamy
effect, like a motion picture in slow motion," Lind acknowl-
edges an aspect of Faulkner's work seldom recognized by literary critics—its connections with films and filmmaking.

Although Faulkner spent many years in Hollywood, collab-
orating on nearly fifty films and associating with many people
in the movie industry, scholars and critics have given little attention to cinematic aspects in analyzing his works and evalu-
ating his achievements. Four essays in this volume, however,
treat various aspects of Faulkner's relation to film. In "The
Montage Element in Faulkner's Fiction," Bruce Kawin explores
a theme developed in Kenner's essays by pointing out that the
arts of literature, painting, and film went through the modernist
crisis at about the same time early in the twentieth century.
Modernist writers, painters, and filmmakers—Joyce and Proust,
Picasso and Braque, Eisenstein and Ruttmann, among others—
used various types of montage to express the fragmentation
they saw in the world around them. By observing that the
montage archetype was not restricted to films but was pervasive

in the culture, Kawin prepares the reader for his examination of five forms of montage he finds in Faulkner's writing: the oxymoron, dynamic unresolution, parallel plotting, rapid shifts in time and space, and multiple narration. Kawin does not claim that the source of Faulkner's use of these techniques was Eisenstein rather than Joyce, but he does stress the aesthetic and technical unity of literature and film in order to show that Faulkner used methods also found in the cinema. In so doing, Kawin helps us understand many elements of Faulkner's writing. He also helps us appreciate Faulkner's contributions to the culture of the twentieth century, for Kawin reveals that Faulkner, through his impact on New Wave cinema, has influenced film as profoundly as he has influenced modern literature. For his second essay, "Faulkner's Film Career: The Years with Hawks," Kawin turns from Faulkner's "cinematic novels" to his screenplays. He demonstrates that all of the writing Faulkner did in Hollywood was not simply hack work. Since many of Faulkner's screenplays are quite good and are closely related to the themes of his major fiction, Kawin urges that these be published so that the full range of his career can be appreciated and enjoyed.

A third aspect of Faulkner and film—cinematic adaptations of his fiction—is described in two essays by Horton Foote. In "On First Dramatizing Faulkner," Foote describes his experiences in writing "The Old Man" for television. He also explains why many adaptations of Faulkner's works have been disappointing: "Hollywood has so often failed with him because they insisted on improving him—for whatever reasons: to make him more palatable, more popular, more commercial." Foote's experiences in dramatizing a story from *Knight's Gambit* are recounted in "*Tomorrow*: The Genesis of a Screenplay." Foote first wrote *Tomorrow* for television and later revised it for a stage production starring Robert Duvall and Olga Bellin. These actors later appeared in the film version of *Tomorrow*, which is widely acknowledged as the best adaptation of a Faulkner story for the screen and for which Foote wrote the script.

The 1978 Faulkner and Yoknapatawpha Conference featured the lectures printed here as well as discussions of "Faulkner and Film," "Faulkner the Artist," and "Faulkner the Man"; tours of Oxford and Lafayette County; slide presentations by J. M. Faulkner, Jo Marshall, and Eva Miller; and an exhibit of books on William Faulkner submitted by various university presses and hosted by the University Press of Mississippi. Other special events included an early birthday celebration for Malcolm Cowley (he was 80 on August 24, 1978); an exhibition of watercolors, "Impressions of Faulkner Country," by William C. Baggett, Jr.; and a display from Carl Petersen's collection of items relating to Faulkner's Hollywood years. Displayed were many items described in Petersen's *Each in Its Ordered Place: A Faulkner Collector's Notebook*: scripts, stills, posters, and reviews of Faulkner films and adaptations; Faulkner's first contract as a screenwriter with Metro-Goldwyn-Mayer; and the MGM telegram firing the Nobel prize-winning author. *Tomorrow* and two films on which Faulkner collaborated, *Today We Live* and *The Road to Glory*, were shown along with film interviews with Howard Hawks and others who knew Faulkner in Hollywood. Will Geer, who played the sheriff in *Intruder in the Dust* and the grandfather in *The Reivers*, was scheduled to present dramatic readings of his favorite passages from Faulkner's novels. Three months before the conference began, Geer died. To his memory this volume is dedicated.

In addition to acknowledging appreciation to the many persons who contributed to the conference out of which this volume grew, the editors offer special thanks to the following individuals and groups: Chancellor Porter L. Fortune, Jr., James W. Webb, Carl Petersen, Jody Jaeger and the Mississippi Authority for Educational Television, members of the Faulkner Conference Committee, faculty and students of the English

Department, and the staffs of the Division of Continuing Education, the university library, the university museums, the University Foundation, and the University Press of Mississippi.

ANN J. ABADIE
UNIVERSITY OF MISSISSIPPI
OXFORD, MISSISSIPPI

Faulkner, Modernism, and Film:
Faulkner and Yoknapatawpha,
1978

# Magic in Faulkner

MALCOLM COWLEY

In April, 1953, when Faulkner was trying to finish his ambitious novel *A Fable*, he wrote a significant letter to his friend Joan Williams.

Working at the big book [he said]. . . . I know now—believe now—that this may be the last major, ambitious work; there will be short things, of course. The stuff is still good, but I know now that I am getting toward the end, the bottom of the barrel. The stuff is still good, but I know now that there is not very much more of it, a little trash comes up constantly now, which must be sifted out. And now, at last, I have some perspective on all I have done. I mean, the work apart from me, the work which I did apart from what I am. . . . And now I realize for the first time what an amazing gift I had: uneducated in every formal sense, without even very literate, let alone literary, companions, yet to have made the things I made. I dont know where it came from. I dont know why God or gods or whoever it was, selected me to be the vessel. Believe me, this is not humility, false modesty: it is simply amazement. I wonder if you have ever had that thought about the work and the country man whom you know as Bill Faulkner—what little connection there seems to be between them.

Faulkner's work, so different from the daily character of Bill Faulkner the countryman, has been the subject of a vast and still growing body of scholarship. It has been described, analyzed, explicated, diagramed, concorded, indexed, praised,

3

condemned, or exalted in an uncounted number of monographs, dissertations, and scholarly papers, most of which can be consulted in the Mississippi Room of the university library. But there is one question, at least, to which this army of critics and scholars has failed to give adequate answers—for of course there is more than one answer. Why has Faulkner's work the power to call forth this overwhelming response—not from all readers, of course, but from a devoted body of readers and scholars? What is the source and nature of Faulkner's magic?

Tonight I should like to offer one answer to that question. It is not, I repeat, the only answer, but still it helps to explain one source of Faulkner's power. His work appeals to something deep in his readers because he is a great mythopoeist, or mythmaker. He became a great mythmaker because, more than any other American author since Melville, he was able to use the rich resources of his unconscious, while combining them with his sharp conscious observations and retentive memory of everything he experienced.

A myth, according to *Webster's Collegiate Dictionary*, is "a usually traditional story of ostensibly historical events that serves to unfold part of the world view of a people or explain a practice, belief or natural phenomenon." That is a serviceable definition, but it omits many elements of myths in a broader sense. Mythical characters seem larger than ordinary people. They may be gods, heroes, ancestors, villains, monsters; they may be holy fools, wise old men or women, princesses, loyal retainers, or outcasts, but they always move against the background of a human community, or of the sometimes inhuman wilderness. The story often involves superhuman or magical elements, but in any case it follows a ritual pattern, with the successive events taking place, not by the usual laws of cause and effect, but because they are preordained.

Myths all over the world have an astonishing similarity, possibly—or so it is conjectured by many anthropologists—because they correspond to patterns preexisting in the human unconscious. They are almost always full of objects and incidents that have a symbolic value of the sort that psychologists find in dreams. Trees, forests, rivers, mountains, and strongholds keep recurring in them, as do wise animals, dragons, invincible weapons, magic potions, witches, fetishes, talismans, initiations, deadly perils, descents into the underworld, flights, pursuits, atonements, and sacrifices. Often they exert a powerful effect on their hearers, who feel that they are participants in a sacred drama with an ending ordained since the beginning of time.

The magical or mythopoeic side of Faulkner's work has been passed over in silence by many of his critics. I cite for example Cleanth Brooks, who is perhaps the best of them; surely his two books on Faulkner are the most comprehensive and level-headed. Nevertheless, in his long chapter on *Absalom, Absalom!*, he does not concede that the novel has a mythical or legendary power. Instead he makes the point that the hero-villain, Colonel Sutpen, is not a representative southern planter and that he embodies the Protestant ethic in a fashion more likely to be found in the North. That is a valid observation, but it leads the critic to what I feel is a false conclusion. Sutpen is an alien in the Deep South, *therefore*—Brooks says in effect—the downfall of his house cannot be interpreted as a tragic fable of southern history. Brooks's implied "therefore" depends on a much too literal notion of myths and symbols, especially of those suggested to an author by his largely unconscious mind. Why should Brooks demand that symbols must correspond at all points with events in the foreground of a story? If Sutpen had been a representative southern planter, like General Compson or Colonel Sartoris in the same novel, he would not have been "the demon," as Miss Rosa Coldfield called him, and would never have formed his grand design. There would have been no novel and no myth. Oedipus, for example, was not a representative Theban. In *Absalom, Absalom!*, we cannot doubt that Quentin Compson, as he reconstructs the story of Sutpen's family (not merely of the colonel himself), comes to regard it more and more as having an emblematic meaning and as being essentially southern. So does his Canadian roommate, Shreve McCannon, and so does the average perceptive reader.

When I was reading *Absalom, Absalom!* for a second time, I puzzled over that question of emblematic meanings and I wrote to Faulkner for elucidation. "How much of the symbolism," I said, "is intentional, deliberate?" To make the question more explicit, I quoted a paragraph from an essay then under way. Here is part of the paragraph.

The reader cannot help wondering why this somber and, at moments, plainly incredible story has so seized upon Quentin's mind that he trembles with excitement when telling it and feels that it reveals the essence of the Deep South. . . . Then slowly it dawns on you that most of the characters and incidents have a double meaning; that besides their place in the story, they also serve as symbols or metaphors with a wider application. Sutpen's great design, the land he stole from the Indians, the French architect who built his house with the help of wild Negroes from the jungle, the woman of mixed blood whom he married and disowned, the unacknowledged son who ruined him, the poor white whom he wronged and who killed him in anger, the final destruction of the mansion like the downfall of a social order: all these might belong to a tragic fable of Southern history. With a little cleverness, the whole novel might be explained as a connected and logical allegory, but this, I believe, would be going far beyond the author's intention. First of all he was writing a story, and one that affected him deeply, but he was also brooding over a social situation. More or less unconsciously, the incidents in the story came to represent the forces and elements in the social situation, since the mind naturally works in terms of symbols and parallels. In Faulkner's case, this form of parallelism is not confined to *Absalom, Absalom!*. It can be found in the whole fictional framework that he has been elaborating in novel after novel, until his work has become a myth or legend of the South.

At this point I should like to say, after thirty years or more, that I too was going beyond the author's intention. The truth is that Faulkner's work embodies a number of myths or legends, usually a different one in each of the novels published during his extraordinarily fertile period from 1929 to 1942. Each of the myths has something to do with the South, but is based on a different facet of southern society. But let us see how Faulkner answered my question, in part of a long and revealing letter:

Your divination (vide paragraph) is correct [he said]. I didn't intend it, but afterward I dimly saw myself what you put into words. I think though you went a step further than I (unconsciously, I repeat) intended. I think Quentin, not Faulkner, is the correct yardstick here. I was writing the story, but he not I was brooding over a situation. . . . But more he grieved the fact (because he hated and feared the portentous symptom) that a man like Sutpen, who to Quentin was trash, originless, could not only have dreamed so high but have had the force and strength to have failed so grandly. . . .
    You are correct; I was first of all (I still think) telling what I thought was a good story, and I believed Quentin could do it better than I in this case. But I accept gratefully all your implications, even though I didn't carry them consciously and simultaneously in the writing of it. But I dont believe it would have been necessary to carry them or even to have known their analogous derivation, to have had them in the story. Art is simpler than people think because there is so little to write about. All the moving things are eternal in man's history and have been written before, and if a man writes hard enough, sincerely enough, humbly enough, and with the un- alterable determination never never never to be quite satisfied with it, he will repeat them, because art like poverty takes care of its own, shares its bread.

Reading over those last lines, I could not help thinking of Emerson's adjuration to the ideal poet:

Doubt not, O poet, but persist. Say "It is in me and shall out." Stand there, balked and dumb, stuttering and stammering, hissed and hooted, stand and strive, until at last rage draw out of thee that *dream*-power which every night shows thee is thine own; a power transcending all limit and privacy, and by virtue of which a man is the conductor of the whole river of electricity. Nothing walks, or creeps, or grows, or exists, which must not in turn arise and walk before him as exponent of his meaning. Comes he to that power, his genius is no longer exhaustible. All the creatures by pairs and by tribes pour into his mind as into a Noah's ark, to come forth again to people a new world.

In our own century, Faulkner has been the great exponent of that dream power. He dipped into his unconscious memories as into a barrel, confident that he would find there all the moving stories since the beginning of time, for he shared Emerson's confidence that all human societies, as well as human souls, are cast in the same mold. The barrel seemed inexhaustible, to follow Emerson's phrase, but Faulkner was dipping into it deeper and deeper. First came his childhood dreams or memories, then those of his family and those of the Mississippi settlers, then the Gospel story, which appears several times; then he entered a pre-Christian layer—not only that but pre-literate and prelogical as well, with touches of animism and primitive magic—then finally, as he wrote to Joan Williams, he felt that he was coming toward the end, the bottom of the barrel—"The stuff is still good," he said, "but I know now that there is not very much more of it, a little trash comes up constantly now, which must be sifted out." That was when he was writing *A Fable*, in which he depended less on those subconscious feelings that had served him so well in the novels of the 1930s. *A Fable* was *willed* as a parable, whereas the true gifts of dream and the unconscious must be accepted humbly and sincerely, as Faulkner accepted them in his earlier great books. In these he created a whole series of myths, but the power and magic of his achievement is most apparent in his 1942 book,

*Go Down, Moses*, and especially in that great legend of the wilderness, "The Bear."

Let me apologize in advance for devoting so much of my attention to "The Bear." It has been analyzed time and again and its symbolic or mythical elements have been observed by many critics; I will mention in particular John Lydenberg and Carvel Collins. It is in fact the clearest example of Faulkner's mythmaking power, though it helps us to find the same quality in other books—in *Absalom, Absalom!*, as noted; in *The Sound and the Fury, Light in August, Sanctuary, As I Lay Dying*, and others as well.

Let me retell the story simply as a nature myth. The story (or chapter of *Go Down, Moses*) is in five parts as we know, but we have Faulkner's authorization to omit the long fourth part, which is concerned with another myth, that of the black and white descendants of old Carothers McCaslin. The nature myth is recounted in Parts I, II, III, and V, and here I shall emphasize its magical or supernatural elements, such as extrasensory perception, psychophysical parallelism, reading the minds of animals (as do the old women in fables who can understand the talk of birds), invulnerability to weapons, the belief that objects are inhabited by spirits and that the whole natural world is animate; and, as a special element, a concern with events that happen, not by laws of cause and effect, but in concordance with a ritual pattern preexisting in dreams. I shall have to do a good deal of reading, both to make my points clear and because Faulkner's prose in "The Bear" is truly a delight for me to read aloud, and I hope for you to hear.

Here, then, is the story retold as a myth of the wilderness and a myth of initiation. Isaac McCaslin was first brought into the wilderness at the age of ten.

He had already inherited then, without ever having seen it, the big old bear with one trap-ruined foot that in an area almost a hundred miles square had earned for himself a name, a definite designation like a living man:—the long legend of corncribs broken down and rifled, of shoats and grown pigs and even calves carried bodily into the woods and devoured, and traps and deadfalls over- thrown and dogs mangled and slain, and shotgun and even rifle shots delivered at point-blank range yet with no more effect than so many peas blown through a tube by a child—a corridor of wreckage and destruction beginning back before the boy was born, through which sped, not fast but rather with the ruthless and irresistible deliberation of a locomotive, the shaggy tremendous shape. It ran in his knowledge before he ever saw it. It loomed and towered in his dreams before he even saw the unaxed woods where it left its crooked print, shaggy, tremendous, red-eyed, not malevolent but just big, too big for the dogs which tried to bay it, for the horses which tried to ride it down, for the men and the bullets they fired into it; too big for the very country which was its constricting scope.

Here is the monster of legend: the dragon, the minotaur, the medusa of innumerable legends, some of them going back to the Middle Ages and others to preclassical times in Greece. In this case, however, we note that the "shaggy, tremendous, red-eyed" creature is "not malevolent, but just big." We read on:

It was as if the boy had already divined what his senses and intellect had not encompassed yet: that doomed wilderness whose edges were being constantly and punily gnawed at by men with plows and axes who feared it because it was wilderness, men myriad and nameless even to one another in the land where the old bear had earned a name, and through which ran not even a mortal beast but an anachronism indomitable and invincible out of an old, dead time, a phantom, epitome and apotheosis of the old, wild life which the little puny humans swarmed and hacked at in a fury of abhor- rence and fear, like pygmies about the ankles of a drowsing elephant.

The bear, we note, is the "epitome and apotheosis" of the wilderness; to use a simpler word, Old Ben is the god of the wilderness. As for the hunters who pursue Old Ben, they are depicted almost as a band of priests, each performing his sacerdotal part in a mystery. Ike McCaslin at the age of ten is about to become one of the priestly band, not a full member, but a novice, an initiate. As such he will participate in what Faulkner calls "the yearly pageant-rite of the old bear's furious immortality."

Each novice, if he is fortunate, has a guide and mentor, a wise old man. For the boy in this story, the mentor is Sam Fathers. We read:

> He entered his novitiate to the true wilderness with Sam beside him as he had begun his apprenticeship in miniature to manhood after the rabbits and such with Sam beside him, the two of them wrapped in the damp, warm, Negro-rank quilt, while the wilderness closed behind his entrance as it had opened momentarily to accept him, opening before his advancement as it closed behind his progress, no fixed path the wagon followed but a channel nonexistent ten yards ahead of it and ceasing to exist ten yards after it had passed. . . .
>
> It seemed to him that at the age of ten he was witnessing his own birth. It was not even strange to him. He had experienced it all before, and not merely in dreams.

I shall not stress the sexual overtones of this passage. When the boy enters the wilderness, it is almost as if he were entering the womb. Initiation—so we read in the works of various anthropologists—is a rite of death and rebirth. Did Faulkner read those anthropologists? Possibly he may have done so, for he was a wide reader, but it seems more likely that he discovered some of the same values and the same images by exploring his own subconscious. That was part of his mythopoeic genius.

Old Sam Fathers is the son of a Chickasaw chief by a Negro slave woman. With the blood of the wilderness running strong in him, he feels a mysterious affinity for the bear, and we find him, at points in the story, even reading the bear's mind. Should we call that extrasensory perception? Or should we think of all the fairy stories in which someone is able to understand the language of animals? In many respects, as I have suggested, "The Bear" is like a fairy story.

It is a characteristic of fairy stories that their plots move forward by what we might call a graded series of actions or events, with each event being a little more intense than the one that preceded it. Faulkner also made frequent use of the graded series and nowhere more effectively than in "The Bear." The story contains three or four of the series, but the one that is easiest to recognize is the series of events that leads up to the decisive moment when the boy first catches sight of the bear.

First event in the series: The hounds see the bear, and their baying changes from a ringing chorus to "a moiling yapping an octave too high and with something . . . in it which he could not yet recognize." Later Ike and Sam find the dogs huddled under the kitchen and smell an effluvium of something more than dog.

Second event: With his mystic knowledge of where the bear can be found, Sam leads young Ike deep into the woods and shows him "the rotted log scored and gutted with clawmarks and, in the wet earth beside it, the print of the enormous warped two-toed foot. Now he knew what he had heard in the hounds' voices in the woods that morning and what he had smelled when he peered under the kitchen where they huddled"; it was the sound and the smell of fear.

Third event: On the following morning Ike is on a new stand with his loaded gun. "He heard no dogs at all. He never did certainly hear them. He only heard the drumming of the woodpecker stop short off, and knew that the bear was looking at him. He never saw it. He did not know whether it was facing him from the cane or behind him. He did not move, holding the useless gun which he knew now he would never fire at it, now or ever, tasting in his saliva that taint of brass which he had smelled in the huddled dogs when he peered under the kitchen. . . . *So I will have to see him*, he thought, without dread or even hope. *I will have to look at him.*"

Each of these three experiences is more intense for Ike than the one that preceded it. They are building toward a fourth event or experience that will be still more intense, that will serve as a first climax of Ike's novitiate as a priest of the wilderness. At this point Ike resembles an Indian boy in search of a vision that will shape his future life. I quote from an account by two anthropologists reprinted in *Bear, Man, and God*; they are describing the initiation rites of the Omaha tribe:

Four days and nights the youth was to fast and pray provided he was physically able to bear so long a strain. No matter how hungry he became, he was forbidden to use the bow and arrows put into his hands by his father when he left his home for this solitary test of endurance. When he fell into a sleep or a trance, if he saw or heard anything that thing was to become a special medium through which the youth could receive supernatural aid. . . . He passed through his experience alone, and alone he returned to his father's lodge.

Young Ike McCaslin's special vision will be of the bear. The graded series that leads up to it had started with the hounds' catching sight of Old Ben. It had continued with Ike's seeing the bear's footprint and then, as a third event, with the bear's looking at Ike. Now the boy, alone in the wilderness, must see the bear for himself, but this fourth event requires a lapse of time and a special preparation. It is midsummer of the following year. Ike and his older companions have returned to the camp in the wilderness. Each morning after breakfast Ike leaves the camp with his shotgun, a watch, and a compass, ostensibly to hunt squirrels; actually he is in search of Old Ben. For three successive days he ranges farther and farther into the wilderness, always alone, but always he comes back to camp without his vision. As he returns on the third evening, he meets Sam Fathers, who says, "You ain't looked right. . . . It's the gun."

He takes Sam's advice. On the fourth morning he leaves camp before dawn, without breakfast (fasting like an Indian boy), and leaves the gun behind. Ranging still farther into the wilderness, he searches for nine hours without finding a sign of Old Ben. Then he decides that leaving the gun behind isn't enough. He is still tainted; he still has the watch and the compass. He hangs them both on a bush, and leans against the bush the stick he has carried as a protection against snakes. Empty-handed, he continues his search.

Slowly he realizes that, without watch or compass, he is completely lost. He does what Sam had told him to do if lost; that is, he makes a circular cast to cross his backtrack. He doesn't find the track, so he follows a second instruction of Sam's by making a wider cast in the opposite direction. Once again failure; he finds no trace of his feet, or of any feet. Close to panic now, he follows a third instruction by sitting down on a log to think things over. Then comes one of the finest passages in a superb story, a passage that must be quoted in full:

. . . seeing as he sat down on the log the crooked print, the warped indentation in the wet ground which while he looked at it continued to fill with water until it was level full and the water began to over-flow and the sides of the print began to dissolve away. Even as he looked up he saw the next one, and, moving, the one beyond it; moving, not hurrying, running, but merely keeping pace with them as they appeared before him as though they were being shaped out of thin air just one constant pace short of where he would lose them forever and be lost forever himself, tireless, eager, without doubt or dread, panting a little above the strong rapid little hammer of his heart, emerging suddenly into a little glade, and the wilderness coalesced. It rushed, soundless, and solidified—the tree, the bush, the compass and the watch glinting where a ray of sunlight touched them. Then he saw the bear.

That is the vision for which he has searched and fasted, losing himself in the wilderness. The vision has been vouchsafed because he has followed the instructions of Sam Fathers, the priest of the wilderness, and has even gone beyond those instructions by abandoning watch and compass as well as gun. He has performed the magic ritual and it has produced its magical result, without the least taint of science or logic, but in accordance with patterns that seem to lie deep in the unconscious and that Faulkner has embodied in this story. We read on:

[The bear] did not emerge, appear; it was just there, immobile, fixed in the green and windless noon's hot dappling, not as big as he had dreamed it but as big as he had expected, bigger, dimensionless against the dappled obscurity, looking at him. Then it moved. It crossed the glade without haste, walking for an instant into the sun's full glare and out of it, and stopped again and looked back at him across one shoulder. Then it was gone. It didn't walk into the woods. It faded, sank back into the wilderness without motion as he had watched a fish, a huge old bass, sink back into the dark depths of its pool and vanish without even any movement of its fins.

The bear at this moment is more than a flesh-and-blood creature; it is a vision touched with elements of the supernatural. It does not emerge, but is simply *there*. It does not walk away, but sinks back into the wilderness without motion. The whole passage is full of magic in the proper sense of the word, that is, of effects produced, not by natural causes, but by spells and rituals. At the same time it seems profoundly right to the reader because, I suspect, it appeals to feelings and patterns existing in his mind below the level of conscious thinking.

Young Ike McCaslin's vision of the bear is not the only episode in the story that illustrates these prelogical patterns of

15

feeling, in the manner of a medieval legend or a fairy tale. Another is the death of Old Ben, an event toward which everything else has been building. At last the hunters have found a huge dog, another mythical creature, that can bay and hold him. With the new dog, Lion, leading the pack, they set out after Old Ben on the last hunting day of three successive autumns. Here we note another graded series. On the first autumn, seven strangers appear in camp to watch the proceedings. Old Ben escapes by swimming down the river. On the second autumn, more than a dozen strangers appear. Old Ben escapes once more, but this time with buckshot and a slug in his hide from General Compson's double-barreled shotgun. The third autumn will be the climax. Some forty strangers appear to watch the hunt, "so that when they went into the woods this morning Major de Spain led a party almost as strong, excepting that some of them were not armed, as some he had led in the last darkening days of '64 and '65." In the frantic chase that follows, most of the hunters are left behind. Old Ben swims across the river, pursued by Lion and most of the other dogs, but now by only three hunters, who have also crossed the river. (Incidentally, Carvel Collins was the first to point out the mythical significance of their crossing water.)

The moment has come for Old Ben to die, and his death is accomplished in a ritual fashion, against all the laws of scientific probability. Among the three hunters who are eligible to kill him, having crossed the river, old Sam Fathers is a priest of the wilderness and cannot kill his own god (not to mention that Sam is unarmed). Young Ike has decided that he will never, in any circumstances, shoot at the bear. The third eligible hunter is Boon Hogganbeck, who has never been known to hit anything he aimed at; his gun is useless. But Boon also has a more primitive weapon, a knife. As reported by anthropologists, there was a widespread feeling among woodland Indians that bears, being a special sort of animal connected with very old tribal ceremonies and traditions, should be killed only with primitive weapons such as a knife or an axe. Had Faulkner read about that feeling or did he, once again, recapture it instinctively?

The story reaches its climax. The hounds swirl around the bear as it stands on its hind legs with its back against a tree. Lion dives in and sinks his teeth in the bear's throat. The bear holds Lion in both arms, "almost loverlike," and then begins raking the dog's belly with his foreclaws. To save his dog, Boon Hogganbeck throws away the useless gun, flings himself astride the bear's back, and plunges his knife into the bear's throat. ". . . then the bear surged erect, raising with it the man and the dog too, and turned and still carrying the man and the dog it took two or three steps toward the woods on its hind feet as a man would have walked and crashed down. It didn't collapse, crumple. It fell all of a piece, as a tree falls, so that all three of them, man dog and bear, seemed to bounce once."

The death of the bear leads magically to a series of catastrophic events. Old Sam Fathers collapses; after the loss of his wilderness god he has no more reason for living. Lion dies of his wounds. Major de Spain sells the wilderness to a logging company, saving out only the acre of land where Sam and Lion are buried (with one of the bear's paws in an axle-grease tin near the top of Lion's grave). Major de Spain will never go back to the hunting camp, and there will be no more November hunting parties.

But the boy goes back two years later, as an act of piety. That is the episode beautifully presented in the fifth and last section of "The Bear," once again with overtones of primitive ritual and magic. Ike digs up the axle-grease tin, inspects the dried remains of the bear's mutilated paw, then puts the tin back again. He does not even look for Sam Fathers's grave, knowing that he had stepped over it, perhaps on it. "But that is all right," he thinks to himself. "He probably knew I was in

17

the woods this morning long before I got here." Instead he
goes to the other axle-grease tin, the one he had nailed to a
nearby tree; on the morning of Sam's burial he had filled it
with food and tobacco. It was empty now—

. . . as empty of that as it would presently be of this which he drew
from his pocket—the twist of tobacco, the new bandanna handker-
chief, the small paper sack of the peppermint candy which Sam had
used to love; that gone too, almost before he had turned his back,
not vanished but merely translated into the myriad life which printed
the dark mold of these secret and sunless places with delicate fairy
tracks, which, breathing and biding and immobile, watched him
from beyond every twig and leaf until he moved . . . quitting the
knoll which was no abode of the dead because there was no death,
not Lion and not Sam: not held fast in earth but free in earth and
not in earth but of earth, myriad yet undiffused of every myriad
part, leaf and twig and particle, air and sun and rain and dew and
night, acorn oak and leaf and acorn again, dark and dawn and dark
and dawn again in their immutable progression, and, being myriad,
one: and Old Ben too, Old Ben too; they would give him his paw
back even, certainly they would give him his paw back: then the
long challenge and the long chase, no heart to be driven and outraged, no flesh to be mauled and bled.

What should we call the beliefs implicit in that passage:
animism? pantheism? panpsychism? a sacrifice to the spirits of
the dead? the myth of eternal recurrence translated into spiritual terms? All those primeval notions are suggested, and Ike
himself has become part of them. He has replaced Sam Fathers
as a priest of the wilderness, which, though destroyed by lumbermen, will live on in his mind.

As Ike walks down from the graves on the knoll he has one
more experience that evokes a feeling of the supernatural. He
almost steps on a huge rattlesnake, "the head raised higher
than his knee and less than his knee's length away . . . the old
one, the ancient and accursed about the earth, fatal and solitary

and he could smell it now: the thin sick smell of rotting cu-
cumbers and something else which had no name, evocative of
all knowledge and an old weariness and of pariah-hood and of
death." Ike stands there transfixed, one foot still raised from
the ground, until at last, without striking him, the snake glides
away. Then he puts the other foot down and, "standing with
one hand raised as Sam had stood that afternoon six years
ago . . . speaking the old tongue which Sam had spoken that
day without premeditation either: 'Chief,' he said: 'Grandfather.' "

The reader does not stop to question how Ike had come to
remember those two words of Chickasaw that Sam had spoken
six years before, or how he came to know that one of them
meant "Chief" and the other "Grandfather," those two words
of high respect to be spoken with one hand raised. We are
ready to believe that Ike himself, at this point, has acquired
magical powers. "The Bear" is more than a story; it is a myth
that appeals, like other great myths, to feelings buried deep in
the minds of its readers.

# Faulkner and Joyce

HUGH KENNER

Trying to nail together a henhouse in a hurricane was Faulkner's image, one time, for writing novels. You haven't time, he was telling a questioner, for images and symbols; if they happen, they happen. Similarly, you haven't time for deliberated allusiveness, the kind that draws into its ambit the phrases and the contexts of other writers, ensured of recognizability by meticulous attention to pacing. If quoted phrases get into a Faulkner paragraph it's because he admired them enough to help himself the way we help ourselves all the time to words in the dictionary, not because we are meant to seize the applicability of another occasion in some other book. Cleanth Brooks supplies a neat example from the 1927 *Mosquitoes*:

Outside the window New Orleans, the vieux carré, brooded in a faintly tarnished languor like an aging yet still beautiful courtesan in a smokefilled room, avid yet weary too of ardent ways. Above the city summer was hushed warmly into the bowled weary passion of the sky. Spring and the cruelest months were gone, the cruel months, the wantons that break the fat hybernatant dullness and comfort of Time; August was on the wing, and September—a month of languorous days regretful as woodsmoke.[1]

Omar Khayyám has supplied the "bowled" sky and the month

---

1. Cleanth Brooks, *William Faulkner: Toward Yoknapatawpha and Beyond* (New Haven: Yale University Press, 1978), 132.

that is on the wing; Eliot has supplied the cruelest months; the Joyce of *A Portrait of the Artist as a Young Man* is responsible for weariness of ardent ways. Brooks remarks that the young writer "has not fully assimilated" his models, a tactful way of observing that he has used phrases that pleased him as indiscriminately as he used words that pleased him, words he did not always spell correctly, and that in at least one instance— "hybernatant"—did not even exist. "Weary of ardent ways" no more alludes to Joyce than "hybernatant" alludes to the Latin language.

The author of that paragraph from *Mosquitoes* might well have gone on to develop a style of controlled allusion; but an allusive style was exactly what Faulkner did not develop, and efforts to note his literary allusions in general turn up little pay dirt after *The Sound and the Fury*.[2] He developed his own rhetoric, his own methods; and no more than anyone else's fingerprints are the fingerprints of James Joyce discernible on the surfaces of his prose. So to say what he owed to Joyce, after he had written out his apprentice work, we must step back and take account of methods, approaches, and assumptions; neither the quotations nor the mannerisms Faulkner criticism has randomly noted will tell us much.

We need to ask, of course, what he knew of Joyce, a question on which Faulkner was less than ideally communicative. There is one piece of hard evidence: he owned a copy of the fourth printing of *Ulysses*, given him by Phil Stone in 1924. Stone on that occasion was at his most stiffly sententious: "This fellow is trying something new," he is said to have said. "This is something you should know about." This sounds like someone reconstructing what ought to have been said on what got

2. *Pylon* and *The Wild Palms*, two non-Yoknapatawpha novels, are exceptions; in these, and in the former especially, Eliotic borrowings comport with Eliotic tricks for conferring a sombre resonance on the urban and the mechanical. See especially Joseph Blotner, *Faulkner: A Biography* (New York: Random House, 1974), I, 867–68.

21

identified later as an historic occasion; for Stone it had clearly become historic by 1934, when he wrote that Faulkner was "making use of the new and strange tools which James Joyce has fashioned." The naïveté of this remark is neatly offset by Faulkner's 1932 statement to Henry Nash Smith: "I have never read *Ulysses.*" He did go on to allow as how someone once told him about what Joyce was doing; "It is possible," he said, "that I was influenced by what I heard."[3]

To claim ignorance is a classic interviewee's ploy; William Empson has recalled hearing T. S. Eliot on one occasion comparing the Scott Moncrieff translation of Proust with the original, finding it at some points superior, and on another occasion deflecting a question with "I have never read Proust." Empson assumed that it depended on what you meant by "read," and we may want to invoke the same criterion. Faulkner may have been telling his conscience that after all no one has ever *really* read *Ulysses.* Moreover, reading *Ulysses* through in 1924, without benefit of a single exegetical aid, would have been a job to demand weeks of full-time concentration; it is easy to forget how much of what we all know about Joyce's book has been supplied us by critical industry. Reading *in* it is something else, and *Ulysses* has had a lasting effect on many people before they have done more than read in it. It profoundly shaped Eliot's thinking-out of *The Waste Land*, though in 1920–21 when *The Waste Land* was written Eliot could not have read all of *Ulysses* because less than half of it had been published.[4]

Dipping into *Ulysses*, then, is one way to profit from it, and dipping may well have been a Faulkner practice. His 1956

3. Blotner, *Faulkner*, I, 352; Richard P. Adams, "The Apprenticeship of William Faulkner," *Tulane Studies in English*, 12 (1962), 146–47.

4. The *Little Review* serialization ceased in the September–December, 1920 issue with a fragment of the "Oxen of the Sun" episode, just about midway through the published text. By the time the printed book appeared in February, 1922, these earlier episodes had been much expanded, so what *Little Review* readers saw was appreciably less than half.

statement that Joyce's book should be approached "as the illiterate Baptist preacher approaches the Old Testament: with faith" suggests more veneration than study. It seems to have been kept around as a sacred book; an anecdote of Estelle Faulkner's both suggests this and illuminates a special sense of the verb *to read*. On their honeymoon, she was to tell an interviewer, Bill gave her *Ulysses* to read. "It didn't make sense to her, and he told her to read it again. Then she reread *Sanctuary*, and with *Ulysses* as a background she understood it, she said." This is supposed to have happened in a run-down two-story house near the bayou in the Pascagoula heat of June, 1929, and it's as tall a tale as you'll find in the Faulkner canon.[5]

What you certainly do find, dipping into *Ulysses*, is something Faulkner could only have found stimulating: a variety of textures. Bloom's internal monologue, for example, looks like this:

Looking down he saw flapping strongly, wheeling between the gaunt quay walls, gulls. Rough weather outside. If I threw myself down? Reuben J's son must have swallowed a good bellyful of that sewage. One and eightpence too much. Hhhhm. It's the droll way he comes out with the things. Knows how to tell a story too.

They wheeled lower. Looking for grub. Wait.

He threw down among them a crumpled paper ball. Elijah thirtytwo feet per sec is com. Not a bit. The ball bobbed unheeded on the wake of swells, floated under by the bridge piers. Not such damn fools. Also the day I threw that stale cake out of the Erin's King picked it up in the wake fifty yards astern. Live by their wits. They wheeled, flapping (152).[6]

Stephen Dedalus's thoughts are carried by more contrived and sacerdotal rhythms:

5. The "illiterate Baptist preacher" is cited by Adams, "Apprenticeship of William Faulkner," 139. For the Estelle story see Blotner, *Faulkner*, I, 746.

6. Page references are to the 1961 Random House printing.

## Faulkner and Joyce

His shadow lay over the rocks as he bent, ending. Why not end-less till the farthest star? Darkly they are there behind this light, darkness shining in the brightness, delta of Cassiopeia, worlds. Me sits there with his augur's rod of ash, in borrowed sandals, by day beside a livid sea, unbeheld, in violet night walking beneath a reign of uncouth stars. I throw this ended shadow from me, man-shape, ineluctable, call it back. Endless, would it be mine, form of my form? (48)

And Molly Bloom seems at first glance not to employ sentences at all:

though he looked more like a man with his beard a bit grown in the bed father was the same besides I hate bandaging and dosing when he cut his toe with the razor paring his corns afraid hed get blood poisoning but if it was a thing I was sick then wed see what at-tention only of course the woman hides it not to give all the trouble they do yes (738).

Sampling of this kind—a natural way of exploring *Ulysses*—would have been quite enough to tell Faulkner the first thing he needed to know to set about *The Sound and the Fury*, that by management of rhythm and diction alone three different narrators can be so clearly distinguished the passage from one to another is like transit to another planet. After nearly six decades we easily forget how radical was Joyce's departure from normal narrative idiom. Tricks of speech are a standard novelist's device—Dickens used them, Mark Twain—but we forget how much they are a matter of idiosyncratic pronuncia-tion. English novelists' devices were governed by English ears, attuned to differences of class which were differences of vowels, or disagreements as to whether certain syllables were to be audibly pronounced or not. The ear's way of governing the signs on a printed page by which one man's speech is dis-tinguished from another was apt to involve virtuosities of phonetic spelling; if we respell in a standard orthography the characters so discriminated, we find they are speaking pretty much the same language. Deformed spelling of spoken words is a trick Joyce employs in *Ulysses* almost never:[7] he worked with syntax and rhythm, diction and sentence length.

In *The Sound and the Fury* Faulkner found he needed phonetic means to discriminate Negro speech:

"He sho a preacher, mon! He didn't look like much at first, but hush!"
"He seed de power en de glory."
"Yes, suh. He seed hit. Face to face he seed hit" (371).[8]

But we tell Benjy and Quentin and Jason apart by responding to devices that may very well have been learned from sampling Joyce. What goes onto the page, even when the presiding mind is that of Benjy the idiot, is a sequence of standard English words, demurely spelled and grammatically arranged. These narratives have recourse to phonetic spelling only when the mannerisms of other people are being reproduced. And we not only have not the smallest trouble feeling sure which narrator is which, we are immersed for the duration of each narrative in a climate of mind, utterly individual, which is less a deviation from a standard narrative norm than a system of perceptual habits by which a private world is controlled.

Certain Joycean derivations seem direct and plausible. Jason Compson, a personification of spite, commences his narrative:

Once a bitch, always a bitch, what I say. I says you're lucky if her playing out of school is all that worries you. I says she ought to be down there in that kitchen right now, instead of up there in her room, gobbing paint on her face and waiting for six niggers that

7. The rare exception—"Pilate! Wy don't you old back that owlin mob?" (219)—teaches us its own principle: an Irishman is making fun of an Englishman.

8. Page references are to the 1956 Random House reproduction of the first printing.

can't even stand up out of a chair unless they've got a pan full of bread and meat to balance them, to fix breakfast for her (223).

The short sentence is his norm, its apodictic certainty: "Once a bitch always a bitch, what I say." But let his mind swerve to an object of contempt—she up there in her room, gobbing paint on her face—a long sentence suddenly runs away with itself, heaping detail upon detail, details vividly seen. This trick seems to have been studied from the narrator of Joyce's "Cyclops" episode, who uses it again and again:

> And off with him and out trying to walk straight. Boosed at five o'clock. Night he was near being lagged only Paddy Leonard knew the bobby, 14A. . . . Only Paddy was passing there, I tell you what. Then I see him of a Sunday with his little concubine of a wife, and she wagging her tail up the aisle of the chapel, with her patent boots on her, no less, and her violets, nice as pie, doing the little lady (314).

That narrator, whose name we never discover, is as brilliant a characterization as any in *Ulysses*; and a brilliant transposition of his habits with rhythm and sentence length from an Irish idiom to a rural American was not the least of Faulkner's means for characterizing the equally repellent Jason.

Quentin's monologue on the other hand draws devices from several parts of Joyce's book, as though only the full gamut of the avant-garde repertoire could be adequate to so complex a morbidity. There are brilliant little sentences that catch the look of something: a sparrow on the window ledge, for instance—"First he'd watch me with one eye, then flick! and it would be the other one, his throat pumping faster than any pulse" (97). Or a racing shell moving away downstream—"The shell was a speck now, the oars catching the sun in spaced glints, as if the hull were winking itself along" (113). These reflect one of Joyce's most striking innovations, the replacement

of long inert passages of description by quick inventive glimp-
ses that draw for twenty words on every technical wile. Statues
in a cemetery: "Dark poplars, rare white forms. Forms more
frequent, white shapes thronged amid the trees, white forms
and fragments streaming by mutely, sustaining vain gestures
on the air" (100). Or a hungry cat: "She blinked up out of her
avid shameclosing eyes, mewing plaintively and long, showing
him her milkwhite teeth" (55).

Quentin's visionary moments draw on the lyrical mode of
Stephen Dedalus, composing and quoting: *That quick, her
train caught up over her arm she ran out of the mirror like a
cloud, her veil swirling in long glints her heels brittle and fast
clutching her dress onto her shoulder with the other hand, running out of the mirror the smells roses roses the voice that
breathed o'er Eden"* (100). The hand that wrote this paragraph
has clearly turned the pages of Molly Bloom's soliloquy, where
we learn of the odd effects that can be gotten by leaving all
the punctuation out of otherwise coherent sentences:

Just by imagining the clump it seemed to me that I could hear
whispers secret surges smell the beating of hot blood under the wild
unsecret flesh watching against red eyelids the swine untethered in
pairs rushing coupled into the sea and he we must just stay awake
and see evil done for a little while its not always and i it doesnt have
to be even that long for a man of courage (219).

A man quick to take hints, his mind full of a book he wanted
to write, could have readily absorbed all those methods and
more from *Ulysses* without really reading it. Concentrating,
perhaps, on a page or two at a time, he seems to have seen past
the strangeness of what met his eye to the underlying expressive economy: what the devices were good for, what set of
human and circumstantial limits each defined. A less intelligent
innovator would have used the unpunctuated Molly Bloom
style for his idiot, judging that it had no place in the last rumi-

nations of a Harvard man. But that would have been to obey
the genteel convention that oddities of transcription mirror
class: deficient punctuation, therefore deficient literacy. Faulkner seems to have understood rather that Molly Bloom is no
more illiterate than Quentin Compson is; her sentences, in that
last monologue, are formally complete, and lack ready indica-
tion of where they begin and end because the tide that tugs
Molly toward sleep is reducing her unspoken speech to a level
intonation. An analogous tide draws Quentin rapidly toward
death.

Benjy on the other hand, though wholly illiterate, is ac-
corded verbs, adverbial phrases, capital letters, periods:

Through the fence, between the curling flower spaces, I could
see them hitting. They were coming toward where the flag was and
I went along the fence. Luster was hunting in the grass by the
flower tree. They took the flag out, and they were hitting. Then they
put the flag back and they went to the table, and he hit and the
other hit. Then they went on, and I went along the fence (1).

Though this may reflect hints gleaned from early pages of *A
Portrait of the Artist as a Young Man*,[9] the point of adducing
it is to illustrate the degree of sophistication with which Faulkner approached his job, avoiding obvious sorts of imitative
form. Benjy, whose working vocabulary has been estimated at
500 words, is not framing these sentences in any context we are
expected to imagine. He is talking to no one—whose patience
would be equal to listening?—and "Through the fence, between
the curling flower spaces, I could see them hitting" is not the
sequence in which anyone talks to himself. His ninety-two

9. Cf.: "To remember that and the white look of the lavatory made him
feel cold and then hot. There were two cocks that you turned and the water
came out: cold and hot. He felt cold and then a little hot: and he could see
the names printed on the cocks. That was a very queer thing."

pages set forth fact perceived, remembered, never understood: reduced to words because a writer must use words.

A comparison with Leopold Bloom's monologue is instructive. While many of the words on the pages of *Ulysses* are to be understood as passing through Bloom's mind, Joyce does not scruple to assist with words of his own when an unvoiced image would be the more probable mental event. Bloom sees a magistrate:

> Sir Frederick Falkiner going into the freemasons' hall. Solemn as Troy. After his good lunch at Earlsfort Terrace. Old legal cronies cracking a magnum. Tales of the bench and assizes and annals of the bluecoat school. I sentenced him to ten years. I suppose he'd turn up his nose at that stuff I drank. Vintage wine for them, the year marked on a dusty bottle (182).

He surely *imagines*, does not word, the bottle; it is surely the author who has worded it and inserted the word "dusty." Faulkner has seized on this principle and extended it; unlike the stream-of-consciousness passages of *Ulysses*, which supply printed notation for thoughts that are being transacted in a specified time and place, the three "monologues" that make up three-quarters of *The Sound and the Fury* employ the stream-of-consciousness convention as a way to construct a book that is finally enacted only in the reader's mind, discarding Joyce's convention that inner speech is necessarily spoken somewhere on some occasion, and making maximum use of Joyce's occasional freedom to supply more words than a silent mind would have framed. Benjy is more than a narrative convention; the Compson family needs an idiot brother for thematic reasons, and Benjy's hurt and bewilderment are vividly projected for the reader to share. But Faulkner makes no real effort to pretend that inside an idiot's mind the weather is exactly like that.

What Faulkner does do is assume the reader Joyce assumes,

a patient reader who will gather and store up transient expressive satisfactions, willing to wait, willing to trust the book to declare itself, willing to dispense with authorial explanations, willing to correlate scenes, collate phrases, even read the book several times. Joyce, we may say, invented such a reader, the most profound and durable of his inventions. Innovative works of art, as Wordsworth perceived as long ago as 1802, alter an unspoken contract between writer and reader, and are only to be assimilated when the reader consents to have that contract rewritten.

The first page of *Ulysses* respects the contractual arrangements presupposed by an Edwardian novel reader: "Stately, plump Buck Mulligan came from the stairhead, bearing a bowl of lather on which a mirror and a razor lay crossed. A yellow dressinggown, ungirdled, was sustained gently behind him by the mild morning air. He held the bowl aloft and intoned:— *Introibo ad altare Dei*" (3). We have here a narrator to tell us what is going on, a place (stairtop), a time (morning), a principal character about to shave, a costume, and a line of dialogue. But before the page has ended those contractual arrangements are being subtly altered. The narrator is laconic in the extreme; he is not even telling us where we are. We pick up references to a gunrest and a parapet; the book is some six hundred words old before a spoken question gives us some real sense of location: "How long is Haines going to stay in this tower?" The narrative voice of *Ulysses*, that is to say, will set before us what is to be seen and heard, but will make no further effort to orient us. To read even the most limpid narrative according to this convention is to make what was in 1922 an unprecedented act of involved attention, patient in the fitting together of verbal clues. Introducing innovation after innovation, Joyce in this way gradually, forcefully reshapes the reader; by the time we have read fifty pages we are old hands with the interior monologue, and have learned to visualize scenes from hints and assemble the tensions and motives of characters out of clues. We have also learned that people carry their pasts about with them, and that our attention to what is happening now must also be alert to penetrate back, sometimes years back.

The reader who has learned such lessons is the one Faulkner takes for granted. Unfortunately, such readers remain scarce, and the first instruction readers of *Ulysses* received from outside the book itself was instruction in admiring esoteric systems of symbolism. Stuart Gilbert, in *James Joyce's Ulysses* (1931), set the book forth according to a rigorous scheme which specified, for the eighteen episodes, symbols, colors, organs of the body, appropriate arts, appropriate technics, appropriate Homeric correspondences. For the next thirty years *Ulysses* was the happy hunting ground of questers after large-scale patterns. Nothing *was*, everything *portended*; the book's variety multiplied in a wilderness of exegetical mirrors. It has correspondingly been natural to assume that Faulkner's novels too are post-Joycean chiefly in being mythically structured.

This is doubtful, if only because the mythical structures in Joyce would not have been at all discernible when Faulkner acquired his copy of *Ulysses* in 1924, or even when he published *The Sound and the Fury* in 1929. Joyce assuredly put them there, though he doubtless did not put in as many as have been discerned, but only the most patient and ingenious reading will get them back out, and it is open to grave doubt that William Faulkner had the time or the inclination for such research. The time of a man who writes novels is pretty well filled with writing, and between 1924 and 1929 Faulkner wrote several hundred thousand words. It seems much more plausible that what he learned from Joyce was a set of expressive devices, effective on the plane on which sentences and paragraphs are constructed, and an understanding he could share with an ideal reader. These devices were good for doing one of the things Joyce had done, fitting the workings of many characters'

minds into a rigorous and delimited time scheme, while imply-
ing what they are always conscious of, the pressure of many
years' past, equally delimited, structured, datable.

Fifteen years ago, in his first book on Faulkner, Cleanth
Brooks was at pains to stress Faulkner's fidelity to the social
facts of his region, and also to provide careful tables of such
matters as the chronology of events in *Sanctuary* and *The
Mansion*, ledger sheets for the financial transactions in *The
Hamlet*, the evidence for our fact-by-fact knowledge of the
Sutpen family, the genealogies (with dates, where possible) of
the Compsons, McCaslins, Stevenses, Sartorises, Sutpens,
Snopeses.[10] Though articles had provided details of this order
before, Brooks may be taken as the first major Faulkner critic
to present a coherent account of the novels with an eye to what
happens, not to what they may be said to portend.

And Joyce criticism in the past decade has been displaying
similar preoccupations, equally overdue: the *Topographical
Guide* of Clive Hart and Leo Knuth, which addresses such matters as how Stephen Dedalus got from Deasey's school in Dal-
key to the strand at Sandymount in the time available (by
tram, with one change), or John Henry Raleigh's *Chronicle of
Leopold and Molly Bloom*, which for 280 pages rearranges the
facts set forth by Joyce in chronological sequence, with dates
and evidence. The past reaches back into the eighteenth century, when Leopold Bloom's great-grandfather, Lipoti Virag,
set eyes on Maria Theresa, empress of Austria and queen of
Hungary. It proceeds with incredible density of documentation
down through the nineteenth century, to the date of the book's
action, June 16, 1904, and forward in prospect even to the
coming September 8, Molly's birthday, for which her husband,
after two changes of mind, has resolved to buy her violet silk
petticoats because "She has something to put in them."

10. Cleanth Brooks, *William Faulkner: The Yoknapatawpha Country* (New
Haven: Yale University Press, 1963).

Long mistaken for a projection onto clouds of myth of an ordinary day's events, *Ulysses* turns out to contain the chronicle, extending over three generations, of an immigrant family in Ireland, making their way, marrying, giving birth, keeping to themselves. In its social and its sociological preoccupations *Ulysses* is more like a Faulkner novel than anyone could have guessed until recently: anyone, that is, but possibly Faulkner.

For Faulkner had, we may guess, the sense of style which turning Joyce's pages could discern, beneath a superficial look of chaos, the control, the brilliant exactness; could intuit too the use of Dublin devices for Mississippi novels equally exact in their genealogies, chronologies, viewpoints, time schemes. The clocks that tick for Quentin Compson, the calendar leaves that turn, measure off phases of a nightmare like that from which Stephen Dedalus says he is trying to escape: that which cannot be undone, and which cannot be forgotten: Faulkner's weightiest theme, and one that needs no symbols to help it out.

# Pioneering on Principle
## or How a Traditional
## Society May Be Dissolved

THOMAS DANIEL YOUNG

*The Unvanquished* (1938), one of Faulkner's best and least understood novels, delineates with clarity and vividness the process by which an established social order may be destroyed and, at the same time, suggests the means by which some of the values of a traditional society may be perpetuated. Writing in *The World's Body* (1938), John Crowe Ransom pointed out that "societies of the old order" handed down both "economic forms" (work forms) and "aesthetic forms" (play forms). Both kinds of forms, he insisted, are necessary for the survival of a social order. The economic forms, represented by "such objects as plough, table, book, biscuit, machine" are utilitarian in function. They are the "recipes of maximum efficiency, short routes to 'success,' to welfare, to the attainments of natural satisfactions and comforts." As important as these forms are to a society, however, they are no more essential for the continuance and well-being of a social order than their counterpart, the aesthetic forms: art, religion, manners, customs, rites, and ceremonies. These aesthetic forms, Ransom believed, "are a technique of restraint, not of efficiency. They do not butter our bread, and they delay the eating of it. They stand between the individual and his natural object and impose a check on his actions." One reason modern society is unable to satisfy the wants and demands of its members is its "horror of empty forms and ceremonies, of their invitation to men . . . to handle their

34

objects as rudely as they can," a sure and certain means of "destroying old arts and customs" and "exposing . . . their own solidarity to the anarchy of too much greed." In his uncivilized state barbaric man seized the object of his desire by the hair of her head and dragged her away to his cave where by direct action he satisfied his lustful appetite. In a civilized society man's actions are not those of the savage or those of an animal, but those of a gentleman; therefore his actions are severely restricted by a fixed code which requires that he approach his lady with "ceremony and pay her a fastidious courtship."[1] His desire is not weakened because he must approach his precious object through a circuitous route; instead as she is "contemplated in this manner under restraint," she becomes "a person, . . . an aesthetic object" and the animal lust the man feels is permitted to develop into human love, as *desire for any woman* is converted into the richer, more satisfying emotion of human love, a feeling directed toward a particular woman (33).

What Ransom is arguing, of course, is that a code of manners allows man a way of life much more rewarding than one dominated by the "stupidity of an appetitive or economic life." By extension, too, the social order that cherishes its aesthetic forms as well as its economic forms provides for a higher quality of life than is otherwise available. But of even greater significance is the fact that a civilization is often protected and perpetuated by its aesthetic rather than by its economic forms. Any social order reflects the imperfections of the human beings of which it is composed; therefore it contains within it the involvements, sins, transgressions, and mistakes of its selfish and greedy citizens—all those elements that would destroy it. Since there will be no perfect societies, any social order is always subject to failure. Since man cannot obliterate his own

1. John Crowe Ransom, *The World's Body* (Baton Rouge: Louisiana State University Press, 1938), 31–32. All future references to this book are to this edition and are included in the text.

imperfections and those of the other members of the social order to which he belongs, he must always attempt to hold in abeyance the destructive elements in his society through the use of these aesthetic forms: its codes, rites, rituals, rules, and ceremonies. Only through a society that honors and cherishes these forms is man transformed into a civilized human being.

A social order fully cognizant of the significance of the aesthetic forms existed in the South before the Civil War, but this society fell before the ravages of that holocaust, the most destructive war in our history. In that war for the first time restrictive war—one fought among certain classes of citizens and in a relatively confined area—gave way to a total war, one that involved an entire society. With this crisis, the Civil War, began the dissolution of all order in Yoknapatawpha County, and to the extent that Yoknapatawpha is a microcosm of the Western world, one can see, as the Snopeses come to dominate this northeast Mississippi county, how Western European civilization may be destroyed.

Convincing evidence of the process by which a traditional social order may be dissolved is revealed by a careful examination of the effect of war upon some of the characters in *The Unvanquished*. The novel opens in 1863, a most significant time because Lincoln has just issued the Emancipation Proclamation freeing the black man (and the enslavement of the black is one of the major sins committed by the leadership of the antebellum South). Too, Vicksburg and Corinth have both fallen, leaving all of north Mississippi open to assault by members of the invading enemy army. Colonel John Sartoris has just been voted out of command of the infantry regiment he raised and took to Virginia when the war first broke out; consequently he returns to Yoknapatawpha, raises a group of irregular cavalry (he says to protect the defenseless women and children), and sets about building pens in the swamp in order to conceal his own stock from the enemy.

The Colonel's young son Bayard, who is only twelve in 1863, for the first two years of the war has regarded the whole enterprise as something of a lark and has spent most of his free time playing war games with Ringo, a young black of his own age. Soon, however, the nature of the game changes, for they see a troop of Yankee soldiers approaching. Between the two of them they carry the old family musket, one at each end as if it were a log of wood, and reach a spot behind a honeysuckle vine just as a rider comes around the curve. They cock the musket and fire without aiming and bring down a horse. They run toward the house yelling, "We shot him, Granny. We shot the bastud." Granny, who is Rosa Millard, Colonel Sartoris's mother-in-law, looks at her grandson and asks, "Bayard Sartoris, what did you say?" And Ringo, to underscore what Bayard has already revealed, exclaims, "We shot the bastud, Granny! We kilt him!"

Recovering her composure quickly because she hears a step on the porch, she says calmly, "Quick! Here!"

And then [Bayard says] Ringo and I were squatting with our knees under our chins, on either side of her against her legs . . . and her skirts spread over us like a tent. . . . We couldn't see; we just squatted in a kind of faint gray light and that smell of Granny that her clothes and bed and room all had, and Ringo's eyes looking like two plates of chocolate pudding and maybe both of us thinking how Granny had never whipped us for anything in our lives except lying.[2]

They are startled, therefore, to hear Granny say that there are no children on the place, that she has never seen the old musket the sergeant brings in. Granny is counting heavily on the fact that the colonel in charge of the troop is a gentleman, whose actions because of this fact are restricted. There are

---

2. William Faulkner, *The Unvanquished* (New York: Vintage Books 1965), 32. All future references to this book are to this edition and will be given in the text.

certain things he will not do: He will not doubt a lady's word
and even if he did, he certainly would not ask her to raise her
skirt in order for him to see if anything or anybody is hidden
beneath it.

Rosa Millard is forced, therefore, to violate her code of
honor to protect the two boys. She is aware that the colonel
knows exactly where her grandson and Ringo are but she
realizes, too, that she has an advantage over the Union officer.
Because of the code under which he is operating, Colonel Dick
is not allowed to embarrass a lady. So Rosa violates the code,
and the error of her behavior is not obliterated, as we shall see,
even after she, Ringo, and Bayard have attempted to wash
away their lies and improper language with harsh lye soap.

The times are so badly out of joint that Rosa Millard cannot
keep the family together without violating the traditional code
again. Her property has been stolen or has strayed away from
home, and she sets about trying to retrieve it. First, Loosh, one
of the Sartoris slaves, tells a Yankee patrol where the family
silver is buried, then having heard he has been freed by proclamation of the president of the United States—or, as he expresses
it, "God's own angel proclamated me free and gonter general
me to Jordon"—he takes his wife Philadelphy and wanders off
in search of Jordan. These events follow closely the loss of the
two Sartoris mules, Old Hundred and Tinney, taken by a Yankee cavalry patrol while Rosa and the two boys are on their
way to Memphis. So Rosa sets out in search of Colonel Dick,
who though a Yankee is a gentleman and will certainly return
to a lady property that rightfully belongs to her. She finds
Colonel Dick when he is confronted with the baffling military
problem of trying to get his troops across a rain-swollen and
log-filled river and then destroying the bridge in order to escape the hordes of dazed freedmen seeking the promised land
that lies across Jordan. She finds the harried colonel, explains
her problem to him, and he asks her to describe her stolen

property. It includes, she says, "a chest of silver tied with hemp rope. The rope was new. Two darkies, Loosh and Philadelphy. The mules, Old Hundred and Tinney" (125). In the clamor and confusion of dozens of people demanding immediate solutions to insoluble problems, the colonel asks his orderly if he has a written account of the lady's request and he says he has. He has written:

Field Headquarters
—th Army Corps,
Department of Tennessee
August 14, 1863

TO ALL BRIGADE, REGIMENTAL AND OTHER COMMANDERS:

You will see that bearer is repossessed in full of the following property, to wit: Ten (10) chests tied with hemp rope and containing silver. One hundred ten (110) mules captured loose near Philadelphia in Mississippi. One hundred ten (110) Negroes of both sexes belonging to and having strayed from the same locality.

You will further see that bearer is supplied with necessary food and forage to expedite his passage to his destination.

By order of the General Commanding.

Although Uncle Buck has warned Bayard that he is now "the" Sartoris and must protect Rosa and the people on the plantation in the Colonel's absence, it is Ringo, who Colonel Sartoris has repeatedly said is smarter than Bayard, who assumes the position of leadership. When Granny is reluctant to accept the additional mules, those that don't belong to her because she acquired them through the enemy's error, Ringo attempts to soothe her conscience by saying, "Hit was the paper that lied; hit wasn't us." But Granny says, "The paper says a hundred and ten. We have a hundred and twenty-two." Even though Ringo protests, "They stole them before we did," she insists: "But we lied, . . . Kneel down." Again, she has violated a stipulation of the traditional code that gives order and direction to her life. She has taken property that does not belong to her, but, she reasons, she has not deliberately stolen it; it has come to her through accident, good fortune, or maybe by an act of Providence.

Rosa Millard's next violation of the code is even more serious than the first two aberrations were. She is not taking an unfair advantage of a gentleman in order to protect her grandson and his playmate, nor is she accepting property that fell into her hands through a stroke of good fortune. She has entered into a scheme with Ringo and Ab Snopes through which she steals horses from the enemy and sells back to him those whose identifying brands can be altered. Her only excuse for her actions is that she is not stealing for personal profit. The money she gets from the stolen mules she divides among her neighbors, and the mules whose brands she cannot change she distributes among her neighbors to replace the animals the enemy has stolen from them. Her reasoning is obviously pragmatic. Desirable results justify any means necessary to effect them. But, I repeat, unrestricted war has driven her to the same unscrupulous means the enemy is using in order to protect herself and her friends and neighbors from inevitable extinction. Rosa Millard's prayer indicates the degree of her contriteness for the sins she has committed. She does not cringe, nor ask for mercy or forgiveness; her prayer, as Cleanth Brooks has pointed out, is "notably lacking in awe and reverence and humility."[3]

I have sinned [she prays]. I have borne false witness against my neighbor . . . and . . . I have caused these children to sin. . . . But I did not sin for gain or greed. . . . I did not sin for revenge. I defy You or anyone to say I did. I sinned first for justice and after that first time I sinned for more than justice; I sinned for the sake of food and clothes for Your own creatures who could not help themselves— for children who had given their fathers, for wives who had given

3. Cleanth Brooks, *The Yoknapatawpha Country* (New Haven: Yale University Press, 1963), 94.

their husbands, for old people who had given their sons to a holy cause, even though You have seen fit to make it a lost cause. What I gained, I shared with them. It is true that I have kept some of it back, but I am the best judge of that because I, too, have dependents who may be orphans, too, at this moment, for all I know. And if this be sin in Your sight, I take this on my conscience, too. Amen (167).

That Faulkner would have us know the seriousness of Rosa Millard's plight is indicated by the name of the chapter in which the scheme that she has devised to strike back at the enemy is described in greatest detail. Faulkner calls this chapter "Riposte in Tertio." A "riposte," of course, is the response or parry with which one follows up a successful thrust in fencing. But a "tertio" was a stroke with which one aimed at the vital parts of his opponent, a thrust for which there was no acceptable response. Since this maneuver violated altogether both the etiquette and the spirit of the sport, it was outlawed before the sixteenth century. Caught up in a war in which all rules regulating its activity are disregarded, Rosa Millard is in an impossible situation. Her only response to an enemy who would destroy the society to which she belongs is one that will undermine the structure of that society. The enemy has presented a thrust for which there is no acceptable response. The enemy has determined that any means necessary to win the war are justified, and Rosa Millard is in a position that her only defense against a pragmatic opponent is to become even more pragmatic than he. But in doing so she is compelled to violate and render invalid the basic code upon which the traditional society to which she belongs is based. The code of manners of a traditional society places rather severe limitations on the behavior patterns of its members. If such a society is to function, its members must follow the code. There are definite courses of actions, as one of Walker Percy's characters explains, that a gentleman won't pursue merely because he is a gentleman. But when a gentleman doesn't act like a gentleman, when the social and moral codes of the society are violated, one no longer knows what's right and what's wrong without having to think about it. There are no traditional values to shape and govern individual decisions; therefore the society won't function. Because she knows there are requests a gentleman won't make of a lady, Rosa Millard is able to protect Bayard and Ringo from the enemy soldiers. But to protect them she violates the code governing genteel relations. This violation at the time seems of little significance because it is developed by Faulkner for comic effect, but it is actually a major step along the road to her destruction.

After a time the *modus operandi* of the scheme which Rosa and Ringo have operated so successfully against the enemy— they have retrieved 246 stolen animals—is discovered, and the plan becomes inoperative. As a matter of fact their partner, Ab Snopes, the father of Flem, the scion of the Snopes clan, reveals to the enemy the location of the pen where the mules are kept until they can be sold back to the enemy or distributed to their new owners. Despite Snopes's duplicity, he convinces Rosa, over Bayard's and Ringo's vehement objections, that she should undertake one final venture to raise a stake to be used by her son-in-law Colonel Sartoris in his attempts to rebuild his own plantation. A group of scalawags, who call themselves Grumby's Independents, had appeared in Yoknapatawpha as soon as the last Yankee patrol had left the county and begun to raid "smokehouses and stables, and houses where they were sure there were no men, tearing up beds and floors and walls, frightening white women and torturing Negroes to find where money or silver was hidden" (171). This band has a thoroughbred stallion and three mares, and Ab convinces Rosa that he can easily get $2000 for the four horses. All she has to do to get them is to write out an order similar to those she has used against the Yankees, deliver it to Grumby, and demand the mares. Then,

Snopes assures her, he will take over, sell the mares, keep $500 for his part, and hand her the rest to present to the colonel when he returns. Rosa, of course, makes a major error of judgment; she decides that if Grumby and his band are not gentlemen, they are at least "Southern men" and "would not harm a woman." For this reason, she believes, she is in no danger even if the scheme is unsuccessful. She soothes her conscience—and it is giving her noticeably less trouble as the story moves along—about taking stolen property by saying Grumby has stolen the horses, and she has as much right to them as he has.

A review of the different episodes in which she has been concerned will reveal the gradual but certain deterioration of her moral character. She has one strength which she uses against all antagonists: she is a defenseless, weak, elderly southern lady whose actions are severely limited by the restrictive code of the society to which she belongs. She overcomes her enemy, then, by doing the unexpected, by violating the code that should govern her actions, but, as I have said, her repeated and increasingly more serious violations of this code eventually destroy her. First she lies and takes advantage of her gentlemanly enemy in order to protect Bayard and Ringo. Then she goes out to recover property that belongs to her. When her property is returned to her more than tenfold because of a mistake the enemy makes, she keeps the lagniappe that has come to her and divides it among her needy neighbors. Her good fortune has such an obviously beneficial effect upon the lives of her neighbors that she enters into a kind of Robin Hood scheme—redistributing the wealth, taking from the strong to give to the weak—with Ringo and Ab Snopes. But though her actions veer more and more toward premeditated deceit and dishonesty—and they succeed because her violations of the codes of morals and manners that have always dictated her behavior become more and more flagrant—never have her motivations been for private gain. Her attempt to steal the

43

horses from Grumby in order to provide Colonel Sartoris with the means of initiating the restoration of his plantation is the first example of her committing the dishonest act, of her taking advantage of the code, for personal gain. The deterioration of Rosa Millard is obvious and complete. Her physical destruction by Grumby is merely a function of denouement.

What Rosa Millard does not realize, in spite of her close relationships with Ab Snopes, is that all men are not gentlemen and that there is no way to summon a generalization that will cover the treatment a defenseless old lady may expect from southern white men. The very characteristics that have been her greatest asset in her dealings with gentlemen of tradition— her defenselessness, her utter dependence upon their gentility, the apparent guilelessness of her behavior—prove to be her undoing in her confrontation with Grumby. She is the competition; she, too, is in the business of stealing mules. To him destroying her is worth the effort because she is so easy to kill. When Bayard and Ringo rush into the old abandoned cotton compress where she has gone to meet Grumby, they find her dead: "She looked like she had collapsed, like she had been made out of a lot of little thin dry light sticks notched together and braced with cord, and now the cord had broken and all the little sticks had collapsed in a quiet heap on the floor and somebody had spread a clean and faded calico dress over them" (175).

If time permitted, the same kind of deterioration could be traced in the character of John Sartoris and Drusilla Hawks. When John Sartoris is voted out of command of the infantry regiment he has organized and led in Virginia, he comes home to raise a troop of irregular cavalry. He says he has raised the troop and is acting outside the regulations of the organized Confederate Army in order to give the best protection possible to the defenseless women and children of Yoknapatawpha County now that there are enemy troops in the vicinity. But

44

the motivation for his action may be more complex; he may be acting partially out of wounded pride because the regiment he has raised and outfitted almost single-handedly has given a vote of no confidence in his leadership, and has acted to replace him with Thomas Sutpen, the largest landowner in the county but a man without breeding or background. The real significance of Sartoris's withdrawal from the organized army may be that he has removed himself from the restrictive codes under which wars are fought. He has no authority over his actions now stronger than his individual mind and will. He is separated from Grumby now by the only restrictions that remain: those on his personal behavior that have come to him from the traditional society that produced him.

After the war, when organized law enforcement is absent from the land, he takes the law into his own hands. He kills the two carpetbaggers who are trying to elect Cassius Q. Benbow, the former carriage driver of the Benbow family, marshall of Yoknapatawpha County. Under the rules that Sartoris devises, he kills the two Burdens, whom he has provoked into a fight, in self-defense. He does let them reach for their guns first, but they are no match for him, a trained gunfighter who, like Doc Holliday of Wyatt Earp fame, has developed a trick holster so that he can draw and fire his derringer faster than the less expert gunman can begin to raise his weapon. Then several years after the war when he and his partner Ben Redmond are in the process of building the railroad, John Sartoris comes home one night, and Bayard sees him cleaning the derringer he has used to kill a "hill man, almost a neighbor." Sartoris says the man was trying to rob him, but again his father's motives are not clear to Bayard because, he says, "we were never to know if the man actually intended to rob Father or not because Father had shot too quick" and besides the dead man "had been in the first infantry regiment when it voted Father out of command" (254–55). At any rate the next day Sartoris

45

sends some money to the dead man's wife, who lives with several children in a dirt-floored cabin. Two nights later she walks into the Sartoris house while the family is gathered around the dinner table and flings the money in Sartoris's face.

After the railroad is finished, Sartoris and Redmond dissolve their partnership, Sartoris defeats Redmond for a seat in the state legislature, and then begins to taunt him deliberately, with the apparent intention of killing his former friend and business partner. "He was wrong," Bayard says; "he knew he was when it was too late for him to stop." Bayard realizes the extent of his father's disintegration most dramatically, however, because of the manner in which his father reacts to an event that occurs the summer before Bayard's last year at the law school of the University of Mississippi. The year is 1874 and Bayard is twenty-four. He and his stepmother are walking in the garden when she tells him to kiss her: "So I leaned my face down to her. But she didn't move, standing so, bent lightly back from me from the waist, looking at me; now it was she who said, 'No.' So I put my arms around her. Then she came to me, melted as women will and can, the arms with the wrist- and elbow-power to control horses about my shoulders, using the wrists to hold my face to hers until there was no longer any need for wrists" (262).

As soon as she releases him Bayard's first thought is "Now I must tell Father" because he knows he does not feel like a man should after he has kissed his father's wife. He has enjoyed the erotic embrace of his stepmother, and the code demands that he report this violation to his father. So Bayard finds Colonel Sartoris in the study and faces him, standing on the rug before the cold hearth. After getting his father's attention, he tries to tell him but realizes his father is preoccupied. After dinner he does tell his father, and his father responds: "You are doing well in the law, Judge Wilkins tells me. I am pleased to hear that. I have not needed you in my affairs so far, but from now on I shall." It is then that Bayard realizes the level to which his father has sunk; it is not that the Colonel has not heard what Bayard thinks is a confession of a disgraceful act, but that he doesn't care. The change that the war has effected in John Sartoris's character is clearly revealed in two passages, one appearing near the beginning of the novel and one near the end. At the beginning of the war, Bayard admits, "He was not big, it was just the things he did that made him seem big to us." After the war George Wyatt, a member of the Colonel's irregular cavalry troop, says that Sartoris's difficulty is that he has had to kill too many men, and Bayard expresses his awareness of his father's "violent and ruthless will to dominate." In the past two years, he says, John Sartoris's eyes have "acquired that transparent film which the eyes of carnivorous animals have and from behind which they look at a world which no ruminant eyes ever see, perhaps dares to see, which I've seen before on the eyes of men who have killed too much" (266). Or, in the dominant metaphor of the novel, dueling—the economic form—survives in the New South; whereas fencing—the aesthetic form—expires.

It may be that the Civil War came, as Malcolm Cowley and others have suggested, as a kind of retributive justice for the white man's cheating the Indian out of the land and instituting the barbarous system of human slavery. But regardless of why it came, the result of the chaotic force of this total war was to undermine the foundations upon which the traditional antebellum southern society had been based. Like any other civilized society, it had fought off the forces that would destroy it through strict adherence to a code of ethics, morals, and manners. The violence released by a completely unrestricted war was more than the aesthetic forms of that civilized society could contain. This war destroyed the basic integrity of the individuals in that society, the concepts of family unity essential to any stable social order, and finally undermined "rules and orders, accepted habits and the convention of property" upon which the entire society was built.

# On First Dramatizing Faulkner

HORTON FOOTE

When I first began to dramatize Faulkner almost twenty years ago, the South was still a remote, exotic region to many people in America. Although there had been critical evaluations of Faulkner's novels and stories beginning with the Cowley *Portable Faulkner*, I still felt that here was material only relatively few had discovered.

When I undertook the dramatization, I had not read a single critical evaluation or interpretation of his work, nor were there many people at that time that I knew who had read him carefully enough with whom I could discuss the problems of dramatizing him.

My introduction to William Faulkner was through the pages of the *Partisan Review*. It was right after World War II, and I began to read of productions of *As I Lay Dying* that were done in the French theatre and the accounts seemed vital and interesting. I went out then and tried to get copies of his work but was not very successful. Indeed, there weren't copies available even in the secondhand book stores. About that time a dancer-choreographer named Valerie Bettis was looking for material for a ballet and somehow I found a copy of *As I Lay Dying*, read it, and brought it to Miss Bettis, telling her that I thought it would be quite a remarkable thing for her to work on. She read it, liked it, and decided to do a ballet for her company based on the novel.

# On First Dramatizing Faulkner

I had met Malcolm Cowley and I knew that he was a friend of Faulkner's, and so I wrote him for Miss Bettis, and he graciously consented to contact Faulkner who gave his permission for her to do the ballet. This was, though in a very passive way, my first theatrical experience with Faulkner. I was not a member of Miss Bettis's company, but I was very close to her and attended many rehearsals and saw the whole work evolve, and I soon realized the enormous theatrical potential in his work.

The ballet was a great success for Miss Bettis and her company and she performed it for many, many years. I then began to find other novels and stories of Faulkner's to read—I forget the chronology of them, but I think I read next *The Sound and the Fury, The Hamlet,* and *Go Down, Moses.* I soon became an avid reader of his novels and stories and considered myself in some measure a student of his then existing work.

I continued with my own writing and became associated through the Philco-Goodyear Playhouse with a producer-director who was born in Mississippi—Fred Coe. He had begun a program called "Playwrights '56" and called me one day and asked if I had read *The Sound and the Fury.* I said I had and he asked if I would like to dramatize it. I asked the proposed time for the dramatization, and he said we would have an hour on the air which really meant, after commercials and station announcements, about forty-eight minutes. When I reread the novel, I wasn't sure with all the time in the world how one might go about preserving what I felt were the unique qualities of the work, so I declined the assignment.

Fred Coe was next associated with "Playhouse 90." This was still back in the dark ages of television when its technical facilities were very limited. Video tape had been invented, but it hadn't been used extensively and not much was known about it. Fred Coe called and asked if I knew Faulkner's "Old Man." I said I did, and he said that he wanted me to think about it as a possibility for television. I had never dramatized anyone else's work then, and I was very wary of getting involved. But because of my admiration for Faulkner, I decided to reread it. I liked it, but as you all know, "Old Man" takes place on the Mississippi River during the time of a flood, and the action of the novel centers on how two people manage to survive this terrible ordeal, and I couldn't conceive of a story of such physical scope being done on television with its then limited technical facilities. Still, I was very drawn to the work.

I was very taken by the tall convict, the plump convict, and the woman whom they were sent out to rescue, and I began to find myself thinking a great deal about them. That's always a sure sign for me that the material might interest me as a dramatist, because I'm usually involved first through my feeling for or about certain characters in a work. However, my rational mind kept saying how in the world are you going to get this on what was then called "live" television, which meant that it was shot as it went on the air, not edited in any way, that the cameras could never be stopped, and that the action was continuous and all taking place in a studio with sets simulating the out-of-doors. I thought how is it going to be possible to do a Mississippi flood on a CBS soundstage in Hollywood, California?

I was living in Nyack, New York at that time on the banks of another river, the Hudson, and I used to walk down along the Hudson and think over the problem. Then some instinct said to me that this was a technical problem, let the technical people handle it; if Fred Coe hasn't brought it up and John Frankenheimer, who was to direct it, hasn't brought it up, don't worry with it. Write it like you had the Mississippi River and the flood and let them solve all the technical details. So that's how I began to dramatize my first Faulkner story. I read it, reread it, and I immersed myself as best I could into his particular world—it wasn't a world, of course, I was a stranger to, having been born on the Gulf coast of Texas, in a town which lay between two rivers that flooded constantly. I had grown up with many people in my hometown who had either recently come from Mississippi or whose family had come from Mississippi. One of my favorite stories at home was how Miss Callie Watts, a school teacher, got her brother out of the Mississippi cotton fields to come to my little town in Texas and become a preacher in the Baptist church. The story went that he prayed as he walked behind the plow in the fields and he asked God what to do and God told him to go to Texas and to preach.

Anyway, the task for me, as I began to read and reread "Old Man," was how to bring all these chaotic, disparate elements of this turbulent flood journey into some semblance of dramatic order. In all the earlier scenes between the plump convict and the tall convict, their relationship is quite clear and quite dramatic, but once the plump convict leaves the tall convict and the woman joins him, I wasn't quite so sure of the relationship and how to make it effective dramatically. I knew instinctively that the literal physical area of CBS—the sound-stage we were going to use, although vast by the soundstages of the earlier days of television—could not comfortably hold more than six or seven sets; and since this novel was quite an odyssey—many places and many towns, many points along the river are touched—I had to begin to make, for technical reasons, a decision about what I would use and what places I would focus on in telling the story.

Now for me, drama in its best sense is a form of concentration and often, I have found, whether it's a small off-Broadway theatre or television or whatever, that limitations are often a great asset. One of the great hindrances, if you will, to the theatre or television or motion pictures, is an overindulgence, having too much to choose from, too much to work with. Although I approached this from a purely technical point of view

in reassigning certain elements of the story or combining them
so that I could use a setting more effectively and economically,
it made me through compressing and clarifying to resee this
work as a play, as a television play. No matter what choices I
made for the setting, however, I knew we would almost constantly be surrounded by water, by the Old Man. But I went
along working on my dramatization as if, indeed, we had every
technical convenience, including the Mississippi itself, at our
disposal.

"Old Man" is a vast canvas. The river, the central metaphor
of the story, has an infinite sense about it. The flood gives the
tall convict his chance to escape from the pen, but he doesn't
want this (as the plump convict does); he wants to surrender,
to turn over to someone else the responsibility of the woman
and the child and go back to the penitentiary and fulfill his
duty to society. He attempts to surrender a number of times
during the story, but something always frustrates his doing so.
Each of these attempts, and his being denied for various reasons the grace of surrender, seemed at first interesting to dramatize, but finally, I had to choose those scenes which seemed to
me most essential to the progress of the story.

A series of scenes I felt most important was the stay of the
woman and the tall convict with the Cajun in his cabin. It was
here that I felt the tall convict was really tempted to give up
his mission. He even forgets for a time the obsessive thrust of
the river that was carrying him further and further from the
place where he could satisfy his desire to obey the authorities
and to return the woman. He was happy here at the Cajun's
shack working and fulfilling himself as a free man and indeed,
if the flood hadn't followed him even here, who knows, he
might have abandoned his journey altogether. But again, the
river takes over. His place of refuge is dynamited. He is forced
again to go to the river and find his way back to Parchman.

And, of course, the woman was happy cooking his meals, taking care of her baby. But then she had been content during most of the trip. I never tired thinking of the woman. She was always (and remains so) a delight to me. Her passive acceptance of everything that happened. Always finding something in the journey itself to enjoy in spite of cold, hunger, childbirth under the most horrifying conditions, infestation of snakes, and gunfire.

Part of "Old Man" is told as straight narrative and part is narrated by the tall convict to the plump convict when they are reunited in the prison. I decided early not to use any personal narration, but to head directly into the river and stay there until the journey was over. Faulkner describes the meeting of the tall convict and the woman in the tree this way:

So he lay on his face, now not only feeling but hearing the strong quiet rustling of the current on the underside of the planks, for a while longer. Then he raised his head and this time touched his palm gingerly to his face and looked at the flood again. Then, he sat up onto his heels and leaning over the gunwale, he pinched his nostrils between thumb and finger, and expelled a gout of blood and was in the act of wiping his fingers on his thigh when a voice slightly above his line of sight said quietly, "It's taken you a while," and he who up to this moment had neither reason nor time to raise his eyes higher than the bow, looked up and saw sitting in a tree and looking at him a woman.

All this is preceded by two pages of descriptive material of what happens to the tall convict when the flood overturns his boat and he loses the plump convict. The tall convict is thrown out of the rowboat, manages to climb back in, is struck by the boat across his nose, and after his return into the boat he is seized by the malignant force of the rampaging river and is unable to control the boat at all. And after the woman gets into the boat with him and he lets go the grapevine she had thrown to him to hold the boat in place, the river again takes them over, and they have no control whatsoever of the boat. Now all this is wonderfully visual, but I knew no matter how large the tanks holding the water might be, there were only so many visual effects we could count on so I wanted as soon as possible to establish a specific character for the woman. I made her a talker and gave her a detailed history to try to involve the audience with her condition of pregnancy and her personal necessity in getting to land as quickly as possible. I did the meeting in a much more physically controlled way.

(*The* TALL CONVICT *takes the paddle. He puts it into the water and tries to manage the boat. The boat passes under a tree. The* PLUMP CONVICT *grabs the limb of the tree. He clears the boat boat as it spins forward and then overthrows the* TALL CON- VICT *into the water.*)
*Dissolve to: The bayou. The rowboat is floating along with the* TALL CONVICT *holding onto it with one hand, and to the paddle with the other. He throws the paddle into the boat, pulls himself up with both hands, and falls down in the bottom of the boat with exhaustion. He stays there a beat, then sits up, gets the paddle, and begins to move the boat down the bayou. The rowboat strikes a tree and he is thrown back to the bottom of the boat, and the paddle flies out of his hand, out of the boat, and out of sight. The rowboat is stuck to the tree snag, and he lies on the bottom of the boat in disgust and fatigue. A voice calls out to him.*

YOUNG WOMAN: It's taken you a time.
(*He looks up slowly and sees a* YOUNG WOMAN, *very pregnant, sitting in the tree, looking down at him. She has on a sunbonnet, a calico wrapper, an army private's tunic, no stockings, a pair of man's unlaced brogans. He stares at her in utter disbelief that of all the women in the world he might be sent to rescue, it would be this kind, in this condition.*)
YOUNG WOMAN: Could you, maybe, get the boat a little closer? I've taken a right sharp strain getting up here.
TALL CONVICT: Yes, ma'am.

55

# On First Dramatizing Faulkner

(*He discovers the paddle is gone and begins to look, frantically, for it over the side of the boat.*)

YOUNG WOMAN: What's the matter?

TALL CONVICT: I lost my paddle.

YOUNG WOMAN: No, you didn't. It landed right up here beside me
in the tree. You can get it. Here, catch a hold of this grapevine.

(*She throws a piece of grapevine that twines around the tree
out to him. He takes hold of it, holds the end of the vine, and
warps the rowboat around the end of the jam, picks up the
paddle, warps the rowboat on beneath the limb, holds it
while she descends carefully into the boat.*)

TALL CONVICT: Do you know where the cotton house would be?

YOUNG WOMAN: Cotton house?

TALL CONVICT: Yes, ma'am. They told me to pick you up down in
the bayou and then to go west and pick up a fellow on top of a cotton house.

YOUNG WOMAN: I don't know. It's a right smart of cotton houses
around here, with folks on them, too, I reckon. (*She looks up at
him.*) You look like a convict.

TALL CONVICT: Yeah. I feel like I already done been hung. (*He releases his hold on the grapevine and the rowboat moves out
into the water. He paddles away. The bayou is lined with
treetops.*)

YOUNG WOMAN: A lot of water, isn't it? (*He doesn't answer, but
paddles on.*) I don't think you'd have ever seen me in that tree, if I
hadn't called to you. Flood took everything, our house, barn, chicken
coop, mule, cow. Would a got me if I hadn't gotten up in that tree
in time. My Daddy is a cotton farmer on the Peter Douglas place.
I'm usually out in the field working with him this time of day, but I
haven't been able to do too much work lately, and then, of course,
it's rained so much nobody has been doing too much work. And we
were all sitting around the house yesterday, or the day before, or
whenever it was, because in all this confusion I've gotten all turned
around and lost all sense of time. And my Mama and my Daddy
and my baby brother said they were going to get the wagon and go
into town, because they were sick of sitting in the house and listening to that old rain.

TALL CONVICT: Excuse me.

YOUNG WOMAN: Yes, sir.

TALL CONVICT: You wouldn't have an idea of where we are now, would you?

YOUNG WOMAN: (*Looking around*) No, sir. I sure don't. If I had a guess, I would guess Carolton is back that way somewhere.

TALL CONVICT: What is?

YOUNG WOMAN: Carolton. That's the nearest town to where our farm is. You ever been there?

TALL CONVICT: No, ma'am.

YOUNG WOMAN: Of course, you wouldn't call it much of a town, but we go there most every Satidy. My Daddy and my Mama and me. Until lately, and I haven't traveled too much lately. Yonder come some telephone poles. Does that mean anything to you?

TALL CONVICT: No, ma'am. To tell you the truth, I'm lost.

YOUNG WOMAN: My goodness, I hope you're not too lost. (*She looks down at her stomach.*) I cain't stay out here forever. I'll have to get to land sometime. I wasn't due yet, but maybe climbin' that tree quick yesterday, and having to sit there all night . . .

TALL CONVICT: Just hold on.

YOUNG WOMAN: I'm doing the best I can, but we got to get some place quick.

TALL CONVICT: Yes, ma'am.

YOUNG WOMAN: I just can't get over how quick it all happened. I was lying down on a pallet resting when a man come runnin' up and says, "Get out, the water is comin' ever which way." And my stars, it was . . .

(*The* TALL CONVICT *is hit over the head by a limb from a tree. He is knocked unconscious, and slumps forward in the boat. The* YOUNG WOMAN *is terrified for a moment. She looks at him, not knowing what to do. Finally, she shakes him frantically.*)

YOUNG WOMAN: Mr. Convict. Mr. Convict. Wake up. Please, wake up.

(*She sees he won't revive for a while, so she takes the paddle, looks around for a moment, and then begins to row.*)

And somewhere along, I decided to name the baby and personalize him a little. I first made us aware of her search for a name for him in this scene:

(*They row on a few yards in silence. The* YOUNG WOMAN

*looks over at the Convict, and she seems nervous about attempting conversation again, but she tries.*)

YOUNG WOMAN: Would you think we'd finally come to something? Carolton, or Yazoo City, or—

TALL CONVICT: (*Interrupting*) Do you know where Parchman is?

YOUNG WOMAN: Yes, sir. It's about two miles from Carolton. It's no town. It's just a landing. Oh, they got a little general store there, but mighty little else.

TALL CONVICT: That's where I started from when I went out to find you.

YOUNG WOMAN: I'm hungry. I ain't eaten in I don't know when. When was the last time you ate?

TALL CONVICT: Early this morning. (*The* YOUNG WOMAN *has a little twinge of pain. He notices it.*) Just keep holding on.

YOUNG WOMAN: Yes, sir, I'm trying. (*She looks up at him. She looks bewildered and frightened.*)

TALL CONVICT: Now, we'll get you somewhere in time. Don't worry.

YOUNG WOMAN: Yes, sir, I been trying to recall the names I had picked out to call the baby, but they're all gone out of my head. I knew a girl back home, they never did get around to naming. They just called her "Baby" from the time she was born till now. (*She bites her lip.*) I can't see two feet in front of me. Can you?

TALL CONVICT: Nope.

YOUNG WOMAN: We might have gone past a million cotton houses, for all we know. A million cotton houses and Yazoo City and Carolton and Parchman and Vicksburg and the whole state of Mississippi. (*He continues rowing. If he is listening to her chatter, he makes no sign. She takes up a rusty tin can. She starts to fill the can with water that has seeped into the boat.*) I better start taking some of the water out of this old boat.

TALL CONVICT: Yeah.

YOUNG WOMAN: Help keep my mind off my troubles.

TALL CONVICT: Yeah. (*He rows on. She empties the can and starts to take more water out of the boat.*)

And then after the baby is born:

*Dissolve to: The Indian Mound. It is early morning six days later. The* YOUNG WOMAN *is asleep in the rowboat, holding the baby in her arms. The* TALL CONVICT *is asleep on the ground. One end of a piece of grapevine is tied around his waist; the other end is tied to the rowboat. The man wakes up, unties the grapevine from around his waist. His convict uniform is so mud-stained that it is by now unrecognizable. The* YOUNG WOMAN *wakes up and gets out of the rowboat. The man walks over to the fire that is burning on the mound. There is a can at the edge of the fire.*

YOUNG WOMAN: The baby is sleeping well in the boat.

TALL CONVICT: Haven't you decided on a name for him yet?

YOUNG WOMAN: No, sir. Some of the names started coming back to me last night. Rosita Marie was one for a girl.

TALL CONVICT: Well, you don't have to worry about a girl's name now.

YOUNG WOMAN: No, sir. And for a boy one of the names I had thought of was Gifford. And one was Gerard. And one was Patterson. Which do you favor?

TALL CONVICT: Let me think about it. (*He points toward the can near the fire.*) There's a little rabbit stew left here, if you would care for some.

YOUNG WOMAN: Thank you.

TALL CONVICT: I don't know what we'd a-done without them matches of yours. Those empty shells stuck together make the driest match box I ever saw. (*The* YOUNG WOMAN *goes over and eats some of the stew from the can.*)

YOUNG WOMAN: There are a lot of snakes on this old mound. Time was when I'd a-died if I'd even thought of a snake, but now I don't do any more than kick it aside. I dreamt last night I was back at the farm. There was a whole lot of people come there to hear about my trip. Their eyes were just popping out of their heads, listening to the things I had to tell.

TALL CONVICT: I had a dream last night, too. I dreamt about John Henry.

YOUNG WOMAN: Who's John Henry?

TALL CONVICT: He's the mule they give me to plow with back at the State Farm. . . . it was cold, and I was trying to pull the covers up over me, but my mule wouldn't let me. He kep' pullin' them covers down and trying to get into the bed with me, and when I tried to get out of bed, he wouldn't let me. He held my belt by his teeth and he kept jerking and bumping me back into bed. And I woke up and I was in two feet of water and that boat there was bumping and shoving me back into the water.

YOUNG WOMAN: My, that was some dream. (*A pause.*) I bet you're tired to death of sleeping in that old mud.

TALL CONVICT: No, ma'am. I got no complaints. It's solid underneath. It don't move.

YOUNG WOMAN: How long you reckon we've been here?

TALL CONVICT: Six days.

YOUNG WOMAN: Six days. The Lord created the world in six days. (*A pause.*) I'm feeling rested now. I'm ready to leave whenever you say so.

TALL CONVICT: How about the baby?

YOUNG WOMAN: He's ready, too. Aren't you, baby?

TALL CONVICT: Well, then I reckon we'll start out.

And then at the end of the play when they are about to be separated for the last time:

> *Dissolve to: The Mississippi. A motorboat with* TALL CON-VICT, YOUNG WOMAN, *baby and* PILOT *comes down the river. The rowboat is being towed behind. The* TALL CONVICT *has the newspaper-wrapped package in his lap. He watches the shore attentively as they move along.*

YOUNG WOMAN: My, isn't this a nice pleasant way to travel? The river sure looks different than it did the last time we come this way, don't it?

TALL CONVICT: It does.

YOUNG WOMAN: How are you gonna know it when we get there?

TALL CONVICT: I'll know.

YOUNG WOMAN: I expect you will. You always did say not to worry, that you'd get us back. There were times I did worry, though. Times I didn't, of course. Well, I'm glad you know where we are, because I don't know where in the world I am. If you stopped this boat now and told me to git out and find my way home, I couldn't do it. Not if my life depended on it. (*The* TALL CONVICT *is looking out at the banks as they pass.*) And you think we've been gone two months?

TALL CONVICT: Every bit of it.

YOUNG WOMAN: Baton Rouge. New Orleans.

MOTORBOAT PILOT: (*Calling out to them*) Back yonder aways we passed Vicksburg.

YOUNG WOMAN: You don't mean it? Vicksburg. (*She looks down at the baby asleep in her arms.*) Gerard, we passed Vicksburg a while back. You better take it all in while you can, because we're liable never to pass it again.

MOTORBOAT PILOT: You husband and wife?

YOUNG WOMAN: No, sir.

MOTORBOAT PILOT: Brother and sister?

YOUNG WOMAN: Just friends.

MOTORBOAT PILOT: I see . . . .

YOUNG WOMAN: (*She looks over at the* TALL CONVICT.) You're sure you like the name of Gerard?

TALL CONVICT: I do.

YOUNG WOMAN: Won't Mama and Daddy be surprised to see me come walking up the road with Gerard in my arms. I hope my Daddy has his cotton planted.

TALL CONVICT: I think they're still plowing. I doubt if they'll get it planted for a week or so.

YOUNG WOMAN: Which part of the trip have you enjoyed the most?

TALL CONVICT: Well, I don't know . . . .

YOUNG WOMAN: I enjoyed it all once Gerard was here, and we left the flood behind. I've gotten real fond of a boat. Two months ago you could hardly get me inside a boat, and now I don't feel right comfortable on land.

TALL CONVICT: Captain, I reckon this will do.

MOTORBOAT PILOT: Here?

TALL CONVICT: Yeah.

MOTORBOAT PILOT: This don't look like anything to me.

TALL CONVICT: I reckon this is it.

(*The* MOTORBOAT PILOT *cuts the engine off.*)

MOTORBOAT PILOT: You better let me take you on until we come to something. That was what I promised.

TALL CONVICT: I reckon this will do.

# On First Dramatizing Faulkner

MOTORBOAT PILOT: All right, you're the boss.

> (*The* TALL CONVICT *gets out of the boat. He puts the package on the ground, unties the skiff, and ties the painter to a tree. He helps the* YOUNG WOMAN *and the baby out of the boat. He picks up the newspaper package and walks on down the levee out of sight.*)

MOTORBOAT PILOT: Well, I guess that's all he wants of me.

What I couldn't get and didn't try for was a certain savagery in the story that could only come if one could visually deal with the elements Faulkner did in the story: the flood, the snakes, the burning of the tree to make a paddle, the vastness of the flooded river.

Upon reading my first draft, I felt I had found an interesting relationship between the tall convict and the woman in the tree which in no way violated Faulkner's more austere relationship between the two and that I had used well certain essential comedic elements inherent in the two characters. Still, I knew a vast amount of time was spent on water so I anxiously awaited, not so much the reaction of Coe and Frankenheimer to the script, as to actually when they would first mention the fact of the water and how to solve it. They called from California to say that they were pleased with the script. They made a few suggestions for changes and told me they had scheduled the work and could I be in California for the rehearsals in a few weeks. I met with John Frankenheimer, who has an extraordinary technical mind that likes being challenged by all sorts of technical feats and he seemed more delighted than disheartened that we had to spend so much of our time on water. He explained they were building two huge tanks in the CBS studio and that he was still determined not to resort to tape or to shoot scenes out of sequence but to shoot straight on from beginning to end as in a live television show. He met with all the heads of the departments and got them equally excited about these technical challenges and I felt a great sense of relief. We were able to cast the play wonderfully. Geraldine Page was to play the young woman and Sterling Hayden, the tall convict. We had a little over three weeks to rehearse and shoot it, but the actors and crew were used to working fast and everybody put their full effort into it. I knew that I had gifted actors and a fine director; the rehearsals went very well as long as the actors were running along the ground cloth and the studio markings. But the first day with the actual set—with the water—there was chaos. I understand, though I never verified this, that the weight of the water which had been pumped into the two enormous tanks cracked the foundation of the CBS building, not severely but enough to cause serious concern. Frankenheimer soon realized that it would be impossible under these harrowing circumstances to shoot the play live, and he quickly decided to turn from his original concept and to shoot the scenes out of sequence. I believe that this was the first television show, for good or bad, that was successfully shot out of sequence, and since the show had quite an impact at the time it was done, it did much to end the era of live television.

Now, although I assumed when first working on "The Old Man" that it was very dependent on the visual for its effectiveness, I had a rather humbling experience about two years ago. Peggy Feury asked my permission to do a production of "The Old Man" in her small studio theatre in Los Angeles. I was rather skeptical that anything would come of the project, but I gave my consent. It was a wonderful production. She did a variation of the classic Chinese theatre use of the stage manager-prop man. In her production he was the plump convict and any number of minor characters, setting scenes for us and describing the stages of the river. The tall convict and the woman were in a rubber boat on a bare stage and through their skill and imagination, it soon became the rowboat of Faulkner's story. It was another kind of journey, of course, but a very satisfying one.

## On First Dramatizing Faulkner

About six months after "The Old Man" was done, I again got a call from CBS, and this time the producer was Herbert Brodkin. He asked me to read a short story of Faulkner's called "Tomorrow" which was from the collection *Knight's Gambit*, and I agreed to dramatize it. Since then, I've been asked to read three works that were suggested for television dramatization—*Absalom, Absalom!*, *Light in August*, and *The Unvanquished*—and one, *The Wild Palms*, which was optioned for motion pictures. For different reasons, none of the productions ever materialized and I've just been asked and agreed to do a dramatization of "Barn Burning" for the American Short Story Series.

As I worked on the dramatization of "Barn Burning," I realized how much had changed since "The Old Man"—how many critics in how many magazines and books have written about Faulkner now. He is taught in the colleges and universities, and many films have been made of his stories. The problem now in thinking of his material is how to shut out all these opinions and critical evaluations, how to see the characters freshly, read the stories as if for the first time and to dramatize them as if they had never been dramatized.

Gore Vidal, who much earlier dramatized "Barn Burning" for television, has written:

There are certain works peculiarly difficult to adapt and one is not always conscious at first of what is dramatically viable . . . certain themes, certain seemingly impossible works do not transfer easily from the stage to the camera; for instance, when I adapted *A Farewell to Arms*, I was reasonably pleased with the script. Hemingway is the scenarist of the novel. His scenes are direct and taut, so playable does he seem that for the first time as an adapter, I used actual dialogue from the novel. I was particularly confident that the first love scene in the hotel bedroom would play beautifully. Well, it did not. Hemingway, in his dialogue, so theatrical on the page does not fit easily into the mouths of actors. It is prose dialogue, not stage

dialogue and though the eye cannot always distinguish the difference, the ear does mercilessly, and I have yet to see a faithful adaptation of Hemingway either on television or on the screen which was
as good as the original. On the other hand, William Faulkner, considered obscure by the impatient was much easier to adapt.

Albert Camus has written:

I like and admire Faulkner. I believe I understand him rather well
even though he did not write for the stage." I presume this was
written before Camus' production of a *Requiem for a Nun* in Paris.
"He is, in my opinion, the only truly tragic dramatist of our time,"
Camus continues. "He gives us an ancient but always contemporary
theme that is perhaps the only tragedy in the world. The blind man
stumbling along between his destiny and his responsibilities. A
simple dialogue must be found acceptable to people who are simple
but who have access to grandeur despite their coats and ties. Only
Faulkner has known how to find an intensity of tone, of situation
intolerable to the point of making the heroes deliver themselves by
means of a violent, superhuman act.

People often ask my advice about dramatizing Faulkner. I
think the first essential is to establish the moral and aesthetic
climate of the producers—to be sure the desire to do Faulkner
is a real desire to understand the man and his world and his
work and to try without being literal to find the theatrical
equivalent for this fictional world.

I think Hollywood has so often failed with him because
they insisted on improving him—for whatever reasons: to make
him more palatable, more popular, more commercial. I think it
would be well for any dramatist to give up this approach. He
can be dramatized: he can't be improved.

# Faulkner's Uses of
# Poetic Drama

ILSE DUSOIR LIND

In 1963, during a summer I spent in New Orleans doing Faulkner research, I happened—quite by chance—to make the acquaintance of a Mrs. Sally Dent, who had been a sixth grade teacher in Oxford. One of her pupils was Faulkner's stepdaughter, Victoria (Cho-Cho) Franklin. Among the recollections of Faulkner Mrs. Dent gave me was one which posed a question, the answer to which has a bearing on Faulkner's uses of poetic drama.

Her memory was of a request Faulkner had made of her when she was Cho-Cho's teacher—that she direct an amateur student production of *Midsummer Night's Dream* in the grove, on the campus of the University of Mississippi. He asked her twice, she said; he seemed very in earnest about it. To this day she harbored the feeling that although he accepted her explanation that she felt unequal to it, he was not inwardly reconciled to her refusal. If she was right in her feeling, why wasn't he? Or, if her instincts were wrong, the request was at least a highly interesting one.

Shakespeare had been performed in the grove at Ole Miss in April, 1916, when the Ben Greet Players, on tour from England, came to give *A Comedy of Errors* and *Romeo and Juliet* as part of the celebration of the Shakespeare tercentenary. The event was an important one locally—large delegations arrived from Grenada, Tupelo, Holly Springs, and elsewhere to see the Ben Greet Players exhibiting the new methods of staging Shakespeare which had been evolved by William Poel and H. Granville Barker.[1] Departing from the Irving tradition of emasculated texts and pseudorealistic stage sets, they gave the plays in full, adhered faithfully to the language of the seventeenth-century originals, and restored the fluidity of Shakespeare's stage. On the present occasion, the whistle of a passing train drowned out the entire speech of one of the Dromios, but on the whole the performances were well received. It was such a rendering of Shakespeare that Faulkner apparently wished made available to Cho-Cho.

Amateur student theatricals were so much a part of life at the university during Faulkner's early years that a teacher's reluctance to undertake them would surely have baffled him. In 1907, for example, Stark Young, an assistant in the English Department, inspired the students to perform Sheridan's *The Rivals*, and Dr. Calvin S. Brown, who taught modern languages, directed a student performance of Molière's *Le Malade Imaginaire*. Brown made it his practice to combine language learning with dramatic performance; for the Shakespeare tercentenary he contributed a program of no less than three plays —in German, Spanish, and French. Dr. Milden of the Classics Department in 1915 staged an outstanding performance of *Antigone* with a stark modern stage set. In 1917, Eric Dawson, an instructor in French who also had his students give plays in French, worked with the Devereux Players, a little theater group which presented plays on campus. In 1917 they performed *A School for Scandal* and *Everyman*, followed in 1918 by Molière's *The Doctor in Spite of Himself*, Hugo's *Les Misèrables*, and Rostand's *The Romancers*.[2]

The energies that went into dramaticals on campus between

1. Oscar G. Brockett and Robert R. Findlay, *Century of Innovation* (Englewood Cliffs, N.J.: Prentice-Hall, 1973), 199, 219.
2. *The Mississippian*, 1917–19, *passim*.

1907 and 1920 derived in some degree from the teaching fervor of a strongly committed humanities faculty, but they also tapped a more powerful source—the dynamism of the new drama movement in Europe. Late in the nineteenth century—with Ibsen, Strindberg, Shaw, and others—drama was becoming vitalized as a medium of contemporary expression, and new attention was also being directed to the sources of vitality of the classics. At the University of Mississippi every faculty member who directed plays had come in contact with the movement in some way. Dr. Brown had edited a collection of British drama[3] and had toured the outdoor amphitheaters of ancient Greece.[4] Dr. Milden, who had also studied the sites where Aeschylus and Euripides were first performed, produced his campus *Antigone* in direct response to the quickening of interest in Greek drama in American universities—at Harvard, where notable renderings of *Oedipus Rex* and *Agamemnon* had just been given, and at the University of California, which had just attracted notice with its rendering of *The Eumenides*.[5] Stark Young, from the time he was first hired in 1905, was already composing plays and sharpening his skills as an analyst of dramatic methods. Riding the crest of the wave of the American interest in drama, he became successively editor of the avant-garde *Theatre Arts Magazine* and drama critic for the *New Republic* (1923) and the *New York Times* (1924).[6] Maintaining his ties to his Mississippi birthplace and to his Oxford friends, Young acclimated them to innovative developments in the little theaters in New York.[7] Eric Dawson, who

3. Calvin Smith Brown, *The Later English Drama* (New York: Prentice-Hall, 1898).

4. Conversation with Mrs. Calvin Brown, July, 1965.

5. *The Mississippian*, 1915, *passim*.

6. John Pilkington (ed.), *Stark Young: A Life in the Arts; Letters, 1900–1962*, 2 vols. (Baton Rouge: Louisiana State University Press, 1975), I, XXIV–XXV.

7. Conversations with Ella Somerville, June and July, 1965. Miss Somer-

assisted with the presentation of the plays in French, became an invited guest of the National Théâtre in Paris upon completion of his book on Henri Becque in 1923.[8] During the years just preceding, while he and Faulkner were acquainted, Dawson was steeped in the controversies surrounding the French classical, naturalistic, and art theater.

The height of student interest in drama at the University of Mississippi came in 1920, when the acting group the Marionettes was founded, following the example of the Carolina Players, the Wisconsin Players, and others. By this time the university theater movement, through which much artistically serious drama was produced in America, had swept the country. Faulkner was one of its founding members and by far the most active one, writing two plays, only one of which has survived, suitable for presentation.[9]

It is apparent then, that drama was very much a part of Faulkner's experience of growing up. Various strands were enmeshed in that experience—in the early years the revival of the English and ancient classics; somewhat later, the independent theater movement, and the art theater movement, with its evolution from symbolism to expressionism. Both receptive and creative aspects of the experience with drama exist. What Faulkner receives he gives back creatively, both in the form of the plays that he writes and in his fiction, which incorporates the influence of drama.

Living as he did in an unusual community, one in which

ville herself subscribed to *The Theatre Arts Magazine* at the time. She and her friends enjoyed following Stark Young's reviews and theatrical activities.

8. Eric Dawson, *Henri Becque, Sa Vie et Son Theatre* (Paris, 1923).

9. Joseph Blotner, *Faulkner: A Biography*, 2 vols. (New York: Random House, 1974), I, 295. "He had already finished the one-act play he had told Lucy Somerville about, and the members were free to perform it if they liked. He gave it to Ben [Wasson], who read it with growing unease. The play was so British it was embarrassing." It remained unproduced, and shortly afterwards Faulkner wrote *Marionettes*, lettering six copies.

small town life and academic life intermeshed and where local residents were essential audiences at performances, is it to be wondered that performances seen and talked about should have left ineradicable impressions? Henry James has observed that to be a novelist, one should be the kind of person on whom nothing is lost. In Faulkner's lumberyard—the storehouse of memory into which he reached for a convenient part to build an imaginative edifice—there was, as he has said, Greek drama.[10] As an example of ways to depict an overriding human vice, there was also, long before Faulkner's conception of Snopes, that master anatomist of vice, Molière.

Growing up as he had in such a milieu, is it to be wondered that he was taken aback by Mrs. Dent's demurral? Or that he should have had so strong a sense of identification with Shakespeare? "I can write like Shakespeare if I want to," he said in 1925, in the fullness of powers about to be demonstrated.[11] Phrases from Shakespeare stud his writings; language from *Romeo and Juliet*, *Macbeth*, *Midsummer Night's Dream*, and *Hamlet* echoes in his fiction in recognizable paraphrase. The early works particularly are ornamented in this way, but the trend is persistent. "There are more things in heaven and earth than truth," Hightower says, updating *Hamlet*. Faulkner matches Shakespeare's broad vision by his own cosmic scope. More important—like Shakespeare—he projects a world. All the arts were becoming projective early in the century, some—as the case of T. S. Eliot and Faulkner—with the influence of Elizabethan drama.

Faulkner's first sustained creative undertaking was his unpublished one-act poetic drama, *Marionettes*.[12] The general

10. Frederick L. Gwynn and Joseph L. Blotner (eds.), *Faulkner in the University: Class Conferences at the University of Virginia, 1957–1958* (Charlottesville, Va.: University of Virginia Press, 1959), 172.

11. James K. Feibleman, "Literary New Orleans between the Wars," *Southern Review*, I (Summer, 1965), 76.

12. I wish to acknowledge with thanks permission to examine the manu-

category of drama to which it belongs is the dream play, brought into vogue by Strindberg and Maeterlinck late in the nineteenth century and firmly established in America by 1920. It belongs also to the tradition of the harlequin play, featuring the clown-lover Pierrot as main actor. It is ornately illustrated by Faulkner, with striking pen and ink drawings. On the verso of the title page of the handlettered manuscript Faulkner wrote, "First edition, 1920," indicating that he anticipated for it the success enjoyed by three art theater plays which enter into its conception. The first is H. Granville Barker's *Prunella*, a three-act harlequin dream play first produced in England early in the century and by 1915 popular with American little theater and university players groups. It was now in its fourteenth edition as a printed book.[13] The second is Ernest Dowson's *Pierrot of the Minute*, which after a short run in England became a fin de siècle classic in its book version, illustrated by Beardsley. The last is Wilde's famous *Salomé*. *Salomé* had been written by Wilde originally to be presented in Paris in Paul Fort's Théâtre d'Art. After it was banned in England, following the Wilde scandal, it had a Paris production in 1894. Its greater success, however, was in the spectacularly illustrated volume by Beardsley. As it turned out, Faulkner's own play was neither produced by The Marionettes, to whom it was made available, nor subsequently printed. If rejected by the Marionette Players as unplayable, as seems to have been the case, Faulkner could have found comfort in the knowledge that Mallarmé had had a similar experience: when his play *The Faun*, submitted to the Comédie Française, was rejected as insufficiently dramatic, he

---

script of *Marionettes*, extended by Jill Faulkner Summers, and to express my appreciation to the Academic Center Library, University of Texas at Austin for permission to inspect the manuscript there.

13. Laurence Housman and Granville Barker, *Prunella: or Love in a Dutch Rockliff, Garden* (Boston: Little, Brown, and Co., 1918). C. B. Purdom in *Harley Granville Barker* (London: 1955) describes the unexpected success of Prunella in America, p. 152.

rewrote it as the poem "L'Après Midi d'un Faun." This poem, as we know, was the direct inspiration of Faulkner's own only sustained poem, *The Marble Faun*.[14] The symbolist dream play and the symbolist poem clearly possessed strong affinities.

*Marionettes* is constructed as a play within a play, deriving an almost infinite reflecting surface from the fact that the main character is Pierrot, himself an actor. Its structure makes *Marionettes* a model vehicle of symbolist elusiveness. There is almost no overt action: all is static, immanent. The play opens with a drunken Pierrot, his head on a table, sleeping on the forestage, where he remains sleeping throughout. On the inner stage his dream is enacted, his own part played by the shade of Pierrot. In his dream, Pierrot imagines a lovely young woman, Marietta, entering a formal garden, yielding to his seduction and changing after she is abandoned by him to a creature of latent passion who imagines herself bedecked by opulent jewels and wearing jade fingernails.

Jade fingernails are the emblems of Salomé, and it is useful to know, as we do through such studies as Frank Kermode's *Romantic Image*,[15] that Salomé, as rendered in the art-for-art's-sake tradition—by Mallarmé, Pater, Wilde, Yeats, and others—is a quintessential romantic image, representing many central symbolist concepts. In this aesthetic tradition, within which Faulkner is clearly working, Salomé is the embodiment of motion in the moment of arrest, as before the beginning of her dance. She also represents both life and art—life as experienced directly by the senses (instead of by the intellect) and apprehended as being both beautiful and terrifying; art as a vital force which expresses its influence directly through the senses, exerting a fatal power through the strange beauty it creates. In her own being, Salomé is seen also to be the container of eter-

14. *Century of Innovation*, 123.
15. Frank Kermode, *Romantic Image* (London: Routledge & Paul, 1957).

nal contradictions, the emblem of the rhetorical concept of the oxymoron. Already, as we encounter the word "oxymoron," we suspect that *Marionettes* is not about love so much as it is about aesthetics—Faulkner's chief passion at the time—and anticipate that the aesthetic ideas expressed in it will have application to Faulkner's fiction.

The symbolist dream play—and symbolist drama generally—was determinedly antirealistic. Its goal was to induce in the viewer a special state of mind, an attitude of profound, enraptured contemplation, in which the viewer had a sense that ultimate meanings were being or were about to be glimpsed. The symbolist dramatists viewed realism as a deterrent to the near-visionary mental state their art aimed to induce. Yeats, in his essay "The Theatre" (1894), provided the rationale for such antirealism when he said that "The theatre of art, when it comes to exist, must . . . discover grave and decorative gestures . . . and grave and decorative scenery . . . dresses of so little irrelevant magnificence that the mortal actors may change without much labour into the immortal people of romance."[16] Decoration and artifice, in other words, replaced realism on the symbolist stage.

Yeats was thoroughly attuned to the symbolist outlook; when he began as a playwright, he consulted such masters of modern theater design as Charles Ricketts and Gordon Craig to assist him with the theatrical realization of his ideas.[17] Craig, vociferous champion of the art theater, went so far in his belief that ideal beauty and truth can be revealed only by means of artifice as to advocate the substitution of human actors by marionettes. This idea was not widely implemented, but it is interesting to note that Yeats's *Shadowy Waters* had a mario-

16. William B. Yeats, *Essays and Introductions* (New York: Macmillan, 1961), 170.
17. *Century of Innovation*, 165.

73

nette preformance in Cleveland during the brief period when serious puppet theater had a vogue in America between 1915 and 1920.[18]

All of which has an obvious bearing on Faulkner's choice of a title for his play, *Marionettes*. The concept of willed artificiality so dominates it that even in the stage directions, Marietta is instructed to stand in a slightly strained, but graceful attitude "like a marionette," reinforcing the idea of artistic meretriciousness which governs its every aspect.

Did Faulkner abandon symbolism and willed antirealism when he became a novelist, putting behind him the artistic ideas that he had evolved by the age of twenty-two, when he completed *Marionettes*? The question is a crucial one. Given his belief that "Aesthetics is as much a science as chemistry,"[19] it does not seem likely that he would violate his own principles. His decision to take his own environment as a major subject for fiction committed him to a certain extent to the depiction of a recognizable world, but significantly, Faulkner did not himself believe that subject matter was the determinant of worthwhile literature. Pondering this question early in his career in relation to the problem of what American culture offered an artist in the way of subject matter, he said flatly: "Sound art does not depend on the quality or quantity of available materials."[20] The choice of his own land and culture to write about was a momentous one because it unlocked for him, with but the turn of a single key, the treasure of all his life's sensory, mental, and cultural experience. It is his handling of this substance, however, rather than the substance itself which constitutes his genius. Realism in Faulkner's fiction is a means,

18. Marjorie Batchelder McPharen, *The Puppet Theatre in America* (Boston: Little, Brown, and Co., 1949), 336–37.

19. Carvel Collins (ed.), *William Faulkner: Early Prose and Poetry* (Boston: Little, Brown and Co., 1962), 74.

20. *Ibid.*, 94.

an instrument, an avenue, a way of illustrating or symbolizing the eternal.

In the course of a few decades, symbolist drama evolved into expressionist drama. This new drama was still antirealistic in the sense that it concerned itself more with the ultimate meaning of existence, with the human spirit in conflict with itself, than with verisimilitude dictated by motives of scientific accuracy. In other words, the expressionists' drama was poetic in nature rather than realistic. As compared to the symbolists, the expressionists' concern was with society in the broad sense. Utilizing the recent insights provided by psychology and anthropology, they penetrated deeply into the essence of individual and social realities. The human issues with which they concerned themselves were real, even at times topical, but they approached them without clinical coldness, identifying themselves subjectively with the condition of man they revealed. From a technical point of view, as dramatists, they made daring use of overtly theatrical means in order to create intense effects. They employed artifice of all kinds—exaggeration, distortion, abstraction, masks, every imaginable theatrical resource—to reach the viewer through the senses and emotions as well as the intellect.

German expressionism as a movement peaked in 1918; American expressionism began to take hold in 1920, with enthusiastic proselytizers like Sheldon Cheney encouraging its spread. Cheney argued, in his pamphlet *Modern Art and the Theatre* (1921), that the dream play had become effete and should give way to works in the expressionist genre. He even suggested writing either an expressionist play or a novel which represented different planes of consciousness, projecting them directly, without resorting to a trick device like delirium.[21]

21. Sheldon Cheney, *Modern Art and the Theatre* (New York: 1921), 18.

Such a suggestion comes near to describing the essential plan of *The Sound and the Fury*.

Faulkner gives evidence that he knew of the work of the German expressionists in his writings for *The Mississippian* in 1922. He also expressed there his comprehending appreciation of Eugene O'Neill's expressionistic *The Emperor Jones*, recognizing O'Neill's stature as a playwright from the outset. The plays of O'Neill are a fruitful source of illumination for Faulkner's own approach to fiction, and many parallels between Faulkner's fiction and O'Neill's plays suggest themselves. For example, *Desire Under the Elms* and *As I Lay Dying* explore the profound relationship that exists between a mother and her children, the mother maintaining the family's ties to the home and to the land; *Mourning Becomes Electra* conveys a Greek sense of fate through the psychological compulsions shown working themselves out in three generations, as does *Absalom, Absalom!*

To offer a detailed illustration of parallels between O'Neill's plays and Faulkner's fiction, let us take a single example: O'Neill's *All God's Chillun Got Wings* in relation to *Light in August*. In O'Neill's play the opening stage set shows a city scene at a point where two rows of tenements converge. As O'Neill describes it, ". . . in the street leading left, the faces are all white; in the street leading right, all black. . . . On the sidewalk are eight children, four boys and four girls. Two of each sex are white, two black. . . . People pass, black and white, the Negroes frankly participating in the spirit of Spring, the whites laughing constrainedly, awkward in natural emotion." [22]

The action of *All God's Chillun Got Wings* resembles that of *Light in August* in part, since the plot deals with a racially mixed relationship between a black man and a white woman.

22. *Eugene O'Neill, Plays* (New York: Boni & Liveright, 1925), 1210.

The pair here is a couple who had hoped through marriage to transcend the race prejudice of their environment, but who find themselves tragically unable to do so because the sources of prejudice are unconsciously internalized within each of them. The man's choice of a wife who is white, it turns out, reflects his need to find acceptance among whites. The woman's decision to marry a Negro is her unconscious way of bolstering a weak ego. Secretly, she harbors a condescending pride in being a Caucasian. Her idea of blackness—which she fantasizes as representing a form of libidinous freedom—is distorted and erroneous, especially as far as her own husband is concerned. At the play's climax, in a fit of madness, she seizes a knife and stabs an African Congo mask that hangs on the living room wall. The extreme melodrama of the scene, in which the symbolic mask figures conspicuously, projects the broader themes of the play on levels that extend far beyond those of interracial marriage.

In *Light in August*, the relation of Joe Christmas and Joanna Burden is a comparable vehicle for broad ironies. Joanna Burden chooses Christmas for a lover because she assumes that she will be able to rescue him from racial oppression. By singling him out in this way, however, she exposes him to danger from the community. Christmas, in assuming that a white woman is acceptable to him as a lover, finds that actually he shrinks at every aspect of their intimacy, at coming nearer to her in any role, of lover or husband, either as white or black. The violence and morbidity of their relationship is rendered in a manner that is schematic despite its intensity: it is projected entirely on a plane of superreality. Their struggle is thus a vehicle for the communication of more comprehensive themes than this personal relationship. It expresses the universal desire for belonging as opposed to the impulse to remain detached; the need for control as opposed to an urge toward passivity;

the craving for libidinous abandonment as opposed to the wish to be constrained by the enforcements of moral convention.

In *All God's Chillun Got Wings*, the black-white symbolism, which is so strikingly imposed from the outset, is analogous to the black-white motif that is stressed in *Light in August*. In the novel it figures not only in many important details—in the white shirt and black trousers habitually worn by Christmas, in the "black blast" which issues from his "white" loins as he lies dying, for example—but in several extended rhetorical passages in which the repetition of the words "black" and "white" reaches a degree of redundancy unequalled in modern fiction. The account which Gavin Stevens gives of the erratic behavior manifested by Christmas during the final chase is the ultimate in seemingly superfluous repetition:

But his blood would not be quiet. . . . Because the black blood drove him first to the Negro cabin. And then the white blood drove him out of there, as it was the black blood which snatched up the pistol and the white blood which would not let him fire it. And it was the white blood which sent him to the minister. . . . It was the black blood which swept him by his own desire beyond the aid of any man. . . . And then the black blood must have failed him again, as it must have in crises all his life.[23]

The black and white symbolism is here exaggerated expressionistically to a maximum degree; similarly, distortion and oversimplification of Christmas's motives are used. Gavin Stevens, the speaker in this passage, knows no more about the actual paternity (the "blood") of Joe Christmas than anyone else in the novel; Faulkner, in having Stevens theorize as he does, exploits Stevens's capacity for intellectualizing to his own expressionistic ends. By letting Stevens abstract the ideological theme in the novel, Faulkner, in effect, built into the book a rough equivalent of O'Neill's stage set.

23. *Light in August* (New York: Modern Library, 1932), 393.

An ingenious use of psychological distortion within the novel, again linked to the theme of black-white opposition, occurs when Joe Christmas describes his walk to town from Joanna's house, after a confrontation with her in which the tensions which will lead to the murder are beginning to build. Christmas's mentally disturbed state here causes him to see Freedmantown in such a way that nothing registers for him except "the *black* life, the *black* breathing"; "the cabins . . . shaped *blackly* out of *blackness* by the faint, sultry glow of kerosene lamps"[24] [italics mine]. Smells and voices emanating from the cabins surround him claustrophobically, choking him, giving him the nightmarish sense of being trapped at the bottom of a "black pit." Even after passing through Freedmantown and merely looking back at it, he responds with "drumming heart and glaring lips," picturing this cluster of poor cabins as nothing less than the chaos of first creation, as "the original quarry," as "the abyss," as the "lightless hot wet primogenitive Female." By contrast, the town proper, as viewed through the eyes of his pathetic yearning, is all brightness and order; street lights positioned at regular intervals show houses with lawns and lighted verandas. These houses present, to his wistful gaze, an image of the conventional social life he thinks he has wanted to be a part of, and which is white, as indicated by "a *white* blurred garmented shape, *white* faces intent and sharp in the low light, the bare arms of the women glaring smooth and *white* above the trivial cards"[25] [italics mine]. Faulkner's rhetoric in passages such as these has sometimes been judged as out of control, but the reverse is the case, his manipulation of point of view to achieve distortion being adroit and most innovatively expressionistic.

*Light in August* links to theatrical expressionism in other

24. *Ibid.*, 99–100.
25. *Ibid.*, 100.

stylistic ways as well, chiefly by repeated references to masks. Puppets, shadows, phantoms, and ghosts populate *Light in August* by rhetorical suggestion, sustaining a sense of pervasive unreality—or superreality—in the characters. O'Neill became increasingly committed to the use of masks in the early 1930s, and Faulkner's description of his characters' faces as masks in many instances serves the same function as O'Neill's, i.e., to give representation to the relatively recent discovery by depth psychologists like Jung that human personality has a dual aspect.

Specific references to the theater also reinforce the antirealism of the novel. Hightower at his study window sees "the street framed . . . like a stage"; the townspeople in their relation to Hightower behave "like people performing a play" in which there are assigned parts; Joanna's passion is like something "invented deliberately, for the purpose of playing it out like a play." Oddly, these references to a mock reality have the force of subliminal suggestion, reinforcing the imaginative life of the novel rather than threatening it, for Faulkner by alluding to other arts draws creative vitality from them.

At one point, Faulkner describes an insignificant bit of action—Christmas's horseback ride at night on his way to meet Bobbie—as having "a strange, dreamy effect, like a *motion picture in slow motion*" [italics mine]. This analogy to film expresses the curiously dreamlike quality of the unfolding action of *Light in August* itself, even as it indicates the way that Faulkner achieves this quality through conscious exploitation of such analogies, in a pervasive system of antirealistic references.

While Faulkner was associated with the Marionettes Players during the years 1920–23 as founder and property manager, busying himself with the tasks of hunting up props, arranging sets, persuading the players to try such new things as using an actual car on stage—was he at that time already studying ways of projecting a world in fiction? Or had he been doing it still earlier, on that day in April, 1916, when the Ben Greet Players staged Shakespeare on the lawn?

# Narration as Creative Act

## The Role of Quentin Compson
## in *Absalom, Absalom!*

THOMAS DANIEL YOUNG

Many commentators have pointed out that Faulkner devoted a great deal of time—to some even a disproportionate amount—to the Judith-Henry-Charles love triangle in a story that is ostensibly about the rise and fall of Thomas Sutpen. Despite the fact, too, that Faulkner exerts considerable artistic energy in pointing out that Shreve McCannon and Quentin are both unreliable narrators, their version is usually considered the reliable one—not only of what Thomas Sutpen and his family did (and even the actions of some persons who might not have belonged to the family) but *why* they did what they did. The credibility of Shreve and Quentin to most readers is not diminished by Quentin's deep emotional involvement in the tale he is telling or by Shreve's insatiable desire to make every detail of the story he creates (with Quentin's urging) fit neatly into a preconceived pattern. This desire for artistic unity is so great that Shreve ignores any facts that he considers unnecessary to his sense of structure, and, as Brooks and others have pointed out, he creates new ones as he thinks they are needed. Even Faulkner's insistence that "nobody saw the truth intact"[1] has not affected the view of many critics. They still insist that the conclusions drawn by Quentin and Shreve are more nearly cor-

---

1. Frederick L. Gwynn and Joseph L. Blotner (eds.), *Faulkner in the University: Class Conferences at the University of Virginia, 1957–1958* (New York: Random House, 1965), 273.

rect than are those of the other narrators. Faulkner even indicates, in a letter to Malcolm Cowley, that it is Quentin's story,
not his, that Quentin is responsible for whatever symbolic
overtones the story may contain. Another statement by Faulkner, however, has not been ignored. When the reader has read
all the different versions of what happened in *Absalom, Absalom!*, Faulkner says, he should offer his own view. With this
encouragement, perhaps, this work of art, one of the most
evocative and imaginatively designed novels ever written in
America, has also become one of the most written about. Faulkner even goes on to say that the reader's view—"this fourteenth
image" of the blackbird—might be the "truth."

The reading I offer of this much interpreted novel—feeling
a little like Fra Lippo Lippi from Browning's poem as I do so—
is based on the following hypotheses: (1) that the Quentin
Compson who appears as character and narrator in *Absalom,
Absalom!* is the same youth who had the disturbing and destroying experiences related in *The Sound and The Fury*, and
(2) that the narrative he creates in *Absalom, Absalom!* is vastly
influenced by the impact these experiences had on him. Given
the opportunity and the motivation of Mr. Compson's letter
announcing Rosa Coldfield's death, he and Shreve attempt to
supply missing details of the Sutpen legend and to furnish
plausible motivations for some of the improbable actions of
the participants in that story. Quentin is the principal agent,
therefore, in the creation of a story that gives temporary relief
to powerful emotional disturbances that will ultimately destroy him. The story Quentin creates assuages momentarily the
deep feelings of frustration and despair produced by his un-
manly and ineffectual behavior before Dalton Ames, a seducer
of Quentin's sister Caddy. The story he and Shreve piece together out of the few facts Quentin has learned from his father
and Rosa Coldfield help Quentin to accept momentarily the
incestuous love he suspects he feels for Caddy. As narrator of

much of the action of *Absalom, Absalom!*, Quentin creates a story in which he can participate vicariously as both brother-seducer and brother-avenger.

In August, 1909, Quentin Compson discovers that his sister Caddy is having an affair with Dalton Ames, a young construction worker who has recently moved with his company into Jefferson. (It was not the first time Quentin had known or suspected that Caddy was giving herself to men, and each incident as it occurred had left Quentin more confused, less certain of exactly how he felt toward Caddy.) His confusion is confounded by the fact that he can neither control her behavior nor punish those who participate with Caddy in her improper acts. Once he throws coal at the pimply faced boy who is necking with Caddy among the trees outside their front door. On another afternoon Caddy comes home and as soon as Benjy, her younger, idiot brother, sees her (or smells her), he begins "pulling at her dress," and they go in the house, with him yelling at her and pushing her up the stairs to the bathroom door. There he stops her and backs her against the door, putting his arm across her face, "yelling and trying to shove her into the bathroom" (SF85).[2] By making her scrub with soap, Benjy is trying to remove from her the scent she has applied to attract the boys. Quentin says later that Benjy can smell death, that he knew by how Caddy smelled exactly when Caddy committed her first sex act. On that evening soap will not remove the scent, and when Caddy comes into the kitchen where T. P. is feeding Benjy, Benjy begins to howl. Caddy rushes out of the house; Quentin follows her down to the branch where she lies with "her head on the sand spit the water flowing about her hips there was a little more light in the water her shirt half saturated flopped along her flanks" (SF186). When Caddy sees Quentin standing on the bank, she asks if Benjy is still crying.

2. All references are to the Vintage Edition (New York: Random House, 1954). Pages cited will be given in the text.

Quentin says he is and tells her to get out of the water, but she does not move. He tells her again and she comes out on the bank, and he asks her if she loves the man to whom she has given herself. She takes his hand and puts it on her breast, under which he can feel her heart thudding. She answers "No," and he asks if *he* made her do it, but before she can answer, Quentin promises to kill the boy before Mr. Compson can find out about it. Then, he says, they will take the money with which he is supposed to pay his Harvard tuition and run away together. Still lying on her back, she places his hand on her throat and says "Poor Quentin. . . . You've never done that, have you?" (SF188). She lies there with his head against her chest, and he asks if she remembers the day she muddied her drawers in the branch when their grandmother died. (This crucial scene will be examined in some detail later.) She tells him goodnight and asks him to meet her later at the branch, saying now she must meet someone. He sees her and some man with their heads close together. She tells Quentin to go on home, but he says he is going to take a walk. He goes close enough to town to see the courthouse clock and circles back by the Compson house and notes as he passes that the light is out in Benjy's room. He goes back to the branch and lies on the bank with his face close to the ground so he cannot smell the honeysuckle. After a while Caddy comes back from her date and offers herself to him twice. He tells her to shut up and asks her, "do you love him now?" She can only answer, "I don't know," and urges him not to cry because, she says, "I'm bad and you can't help it."

But Quentin has found out what he wants to know. No longer is the source of his distress a nameless, faceless quality whom he knows only as man. He is a distinct, separate, human creature, an individualized man named Dalton Ames. For two or three days Quentin seeks out Dalton before seeing him going into the barbershop, where he confronts him. But Dalton says they can't talk there and promises to meet Quentin at one o'clock on the bridge outside of town. When they meet at the barbershop, Dalton's only concern seems to be for Caddy, asking two or three times: "Is she all right? Does she need me for anything?" Quentin does not respond but assures him he will meet him at the bridge at one o'clock.

As one would expect from a brother who loves his sister, Quentin is determined to defend her honor in the respected tradition of the culture to which he belongs. He tells T. P. to saddle Prince and have him at the side door, but when Caddy keeps asking him where he is going he decides to walk. He leaves the house walking slowly down the drive, but he begins to run as soon as he thinks he is out of sight. As he approaches the bridge, he sees Dalton leaning on the rail with a piece of bark in his hand, from which he is breaking pieces and dropping them into the water. Quentin comes up to him and says, "I came to tell you to leave town." Dalton doesn't seem to hear him and continues to drop the pieces of bark into the water and watch them float downstream. Quentin repeats his ultimatum and Dalton asks quietly, "Did she send you to me?" Quentin responds that nobody sent him, not her, not even his father; "I'll give you to sundown to leave town." Dalton lays the bark on the railing and with three swift motions, rolls a cigarette, lights it, and flicks the match over the rail. Again he speaks quietly: "What if I don't leave town?"

"I'll kill you," Quentin responds; "don't think just because I look like a kid to you." Quentin's hands begin to shake on the rail and he is afraid to try to hide them for fear Dalton will see how excited he is. Then Dalton asks him his name, saying "Benjy's the natural isn't he?" Again Quentin says, "I'll give you until sundown." Then Dalton asks him not to take it so hard, that if it had not been him "it would have been someone else." To Quentin's question "Did you ever have a sister did you?" Dalton responds, "No but they're all bitches." Quentin can no longer control himself and strikes out at Dalton: "I hit him my open hand beat the impulse to shut it to his face his hand moved as fast as mine the cigarette went over the rail I swung with the other hand he caught it too before the cigarette reached the water he held both my wrists in the same hand his other hand flicked to his armpit under his coat behind him the sun slanted and a bird singing somewhere beyond the sun we looked at one another while the bird singing he turned my hand loose" (SF199). Taking the bark from the rail, Dalton tosses it into the water and lets it float almost out of sight. Without aiming the pistol he hits the large piece of bark, and then two smaller ones, no larger than a silver dollar. He hands the pistol to Quentin saying, "You'll need it from what you said I'm giving you this one because you've seen what it will do." "Again," Quentin remembers, "I hit him I was still trying to hit him long after he was holding my wrists but I still tried then it was like I was looking at him through a piece of coloured glass I could hear my blood and then I could see the sky again and branches against it and the sun slanting through them and he holding me on my feet." Quentin doesn't realize immediately what is happening to him—he does not know he has fainted —so he asks Dalton if he had hit him. Dalton lies and answers, "Yes how do you feel?" Then he offers Quentin his horse to get back home on. Dalton leaves and Quentin, utterly crushed, leans against a tree, his mind completely filled with one emasculating thought: "I . . . just passed out like a girl." When Caddy comes up, having heard the shots and thinking Dalton might have killed Quentin, she says she has told Dalton never to speak to her again. Quentin asks her if she loves him, and she takes his hand and puts it against her throat and when he says, at her request, "Dalton Ames," he feels the blood surging "in strong accelerating beats."

Soon after this confrontation with Dalton Ames, Quentin tells his father that he has committed incest with Caddy. But

87

Mr. Compson knows his son, or thinks he does, and recognizes Quentin's terrible confession for the lie it is. He tells Quentin he should not be upset over his sister's promiscuity, that only a man would put much value on a woman's chastity. What Quentin should do, he remembers Mr. Compson's saying, is to leave early and take a month's vacation in Maine before the fall term at Harvard begins. We know, however, that Quentin does not take his father's advice; instead he spends September, 1909, in Jefferson, because there on one afternoon and evening he hears from his father and Miss Rosa Coldfield, the old maid daughter of a deceased local merchant, the details of the most fascinating and bewildering tale that legend-rich Jefferson can boast of. Like all the other residents of the town, Quentin is aware of the legend of Thomas Sutpen and his family, but in these conversations in September, 1909, with Rosa Coldfield, Sutpen's sister-in-law, and Mr. Compson, whose father was Sutpen's best friend in Jefferson, Quentin must have had his memory jogged; surely he learned some new details.

Miss Coldfield tells Quentin her view of the Sutpen legend because she thinks he might become a literary man and reveal the facts of this tragic story to the world. What she doesn't know is that four months later in a dormitory room at Harvard, Quentin and his roommate will "create" a harrowing tale of revenge, incest, miscegenation, and fratricide out of the few details he garners from Rosa and Mr. Compson. She has concluded, she insists to Quentin that hot summer afternoon, that someone besides Clytie and the idiot Jim Bond, the grandson of Judith Sutpen's fiancé, Charles Bon, might be out at the ruins of Sutpen's Hundred, and she wants Quentin to go with her to investigate. The truth is that Miss Rosa has little to tell Quentin that is not already common knowledge around town. Thomas Sutpen came out of nowhere, without warning, brought with him a band of strange Negroes, and built the largest plantation in the county on land he had acquired from some Indians. When the plantation was barely completed he married Ellen Coldfield, Rosa's older sister, upon whom he begat a son and a daughter. When Judith became engaged to Charles Bon, a law student from the university, Sutpen for no apparent reason forbade the marriage. Then the war came and Thomas, his son Henry, and Charles Bon went off to serve in the Confederate army.

Rosa can never understand, she tells Quentin, why her father allowed Ellen to marry Sutpen, who to her is an ogre; and his children, her niece and nephew, are far from normal. Just before Ellen dies, soon after the war began, Rosa promises her that she will care for her niece, although the niece is four years her senior. A year later, at her father's death, she moves out to the Sutpen place. After the war when Sutpen returns to the ruined plantation—the son Henry has already killed his sister's fiancé at the front gate—Rosa agrees to marry him but leaves abruptly one evening after he has made an unspeakable proposition to her. She returns to her little house in Jefferson, dons black, and lives the next forty-three years on the charity of her neighbors.

It is extremely doubtful, as I have said, that Quentin learns any new facts from Miss Rosa's version of the Sutpens. Most of the details of the legend that she knows—although she is the only narrator in the novel who had a personal acquaintance with Sutpen—must have been common knowledge around Jefferson. But Quentin must have been impressed with the highly subjective nature of Miss Rosa's account. She takes a few simple facts and creates a legend that gives some solace to the devastating wound she feels. Her only possible explanation for the insult Sutpen had given her—he says let's mate and if the issue is male, "I'll marry you"—is that he was a demon, a monster, a devil that rose out of the ground. She shapes the facts to make them meet her own emotional needs, a device Quentin will use later in his own behalf.

Later the same evening, while Quentin is waiting until it is time for him and Miss Rosa to go out to the old Sutpen place, Quentin hears other facts about Sutpen, some which Mr. Compson had learned from his father. Most of these facts are also well-known and need not be rehearsed in detail here. Because he had been turned away from the front door of a Virginia plantation when he was thirteen or fourteen, Sutpen formulated a design. This "design" required that he have his own plantation, complete with manor house, servants, slaves, family, and respectability. First he went to the West Indies, where because of an act of personal valor and a long period of recuperation he came to know and was allowed to marry the daughter of the owner of the sugar plantation he was managing. When their first child was born, it became apparent to Sutpen (for some reason never fully explained in the novel) that this woman, through no fault of her own, could never fit into his "design." Consequently he divorced her, giving her far more than a fair share of their common property, and left. Then in June, 1833, he showed up in Jefferson, remained a few days and disappeared, to return a short time later with a wagon filled with wild Negroes (two of whom were female) and a French architect. Out on the ten square miles he had acquired from Ikkemotubbe, Sutpen, his Negroes, and the French architect set about building the largest house in the county. After the house was built, though it had no windows, doors, or furniture, Sutpen began to invite citizens of the town to come out to drink and hunt or to watch the fights he had arranged between the Negroes or between himself and one of the Negroes. Finally after the house had stood in its unfinished state for three years, Sutpen appeared in Jefferson again, this time with four wagons filled with mahogany, crystal, rugs, and chandeliers. Again, nobody was ever to know where the goods had come from. Immediately after the house was completed, he acquired the last piece of property he needed to be a respectable planter. He married the daughter of a poor but honest and devout small merchant of the town. Then, almost as if he were following his preconceived notion of the perfect plan, Sutpen had the son, to inherit and carry along the family name, and the daughter, to grace his household, to help her mother entertain, and in due time to allow him to enjoy the love and companionship of grandchildren.

His would seem the ideal family, and one which was the result of his own tenacious desire to mold his personal affairs exactly as he would have them be. In 1857 Henry, the son, enrolled at the University of Mississippi, and his second Christmas there he brought a friend, Charles Bon, home to spend the holidays; Bon was a sophisticated young man from New Orleans, several years older than Henry, and a man of mystery, worldly elegant, apparently wealthy, with an ease of manners and a swaggering gallant air completely out of keeping with the atmosphere of a small provincial university less than ten years old. (Mr. Compson wondered how Bon got there in the first place.) When Henry brought Bon home again for a few days at the beginning of the summer of 1859, any casual observer could see that he was attempting to model himself after Charles in every respect, and immediately after the two boys left, Ellen Sutpen announced her daughter's engagement to Charles. Soon after Charles departed for New Orleans, Thomas Sutpen followed him.

The next Christmas Henry brought Charles home with him again, but this time Henry and his father had a quarrel and both boys rode away. Soon thereafter war was declared, Thomas Sutpen became second in command of the regiment Colonel Sartoris raised in Jefferson, and Henry and Charles joined a company formed at the university.

Mr. Compson speculates on what Henry found, when he accompanied Charles to New Orleans, that disturbed him so deeply. "It would not have been the mistress," Mr. Compson says, "or even the child, nor even the Negro mistress or even less the child because . . . Henry and Judith had grown up with a Negro half-sister of their own. . . . No it would be the ceremony, a ceremony entered into, to be sure, with a Negro, yet a ceremony" (AA117).[3] Mr. Compson thinks that Henry waited for Bon to denounce the woman and dissolve the marriage, that Henry objected not to bigamy but to the fact that Bon was making Judith a part of a harem.

As Mr. Compson recalls the facts of the war experience, Bon was commissioned shortly after the war began but Henry remained a private. At Pittsburg Landing Charles was wounded and Henry carried him back to safety. For four years, Mr. Compson insists, Henry gave Charles the opportunity to renounce the New Orleans mistress and child or, as Mr. Compson expresses Charles's thoughts, "For four years now I have given chance the opportunity to renounce for me but it seems that I am doomed to live, that she and I are both doomed to live" (AA119). Both Henry and Charles thought that one or both of them would be killed, Mr. Compson says, thus making unnecessary a decision from either (Bon's is, will he marry a woman who he thinks to be his half-sister and Henry's is, will he kill his own brother to keep the marriage from occurring?). When the war ended, both men were still alive, and the decision was still not made. As Mr. Compson describes the two men riding up to the gate of the Sutpen house, it seems to Quentin that he can almost see them: "facing one another at the gate. Inside the gate what was once a park now spread unkempt, in shaggy desolation, with an air dreamy, remote, and aghast . . . up to a huge house where a young girl waited in a wedding dress made from stolen scraps. . . . They faced one another on the two gaunt horses, two men, young not yet

3. References to *Absalom, Absalom!* are to the Modern Library College Edition (New York: Random House, 1965). Page numbers are given in the text.

in the world . . . with unkempt hair and faces gaunt and weathered." Quentin imagines Henry saying: "Don't you pass the shadow of this post"; and Charles replying: "I am going to pass it, Henry" (AA132). Afterwards, Wash Jones rode up to Miss Rosa's door and yelled until she opened it and then announced in the same tone: "Henry has done shot down that durn French fellow. Kilt him dead as a beef."

A week after Judith buried Bon she brought to Quentin's grandmother a letter which she said she had received from Bon just before he returned from the war. Although the letter was not addressed to Judith and was not signed by Bon—Ellen Schoenberg argues it was probably intended for the mistress in New Orleans—Mr. Compson believes that this letter, unlike the flowery formal effusions sent from Oxford before the war, proves that Bon loved Judith. Mr. Compson is convinced that Henry saw the letter, and its sincere tone was all the proof he needed to persuade him that Bon was going through with the wedding.

These are the essential facts Quentin has of the Sutpen story when he accompanies Rosa Coldfield out to the old decayed mansion on that September evening of 1909. On their journey out that evening Miss Rosa says that when she learned that Henry had killed Charles, she went immediately to the Sutpen place. She brushed past Clytie (Judith's black half-sister) and found Judith standing in the door holding in her hand a photograph that she had given Bon. (She also says that she never saw Bon alive.) Seven months later Sutpen returned and three months after his return, he and Rosa were engaged. Then one day there was the "death of hope and love, of pride and principle, the death of everything" (AA168). Sutpen returned to the house and spoke the "outrageous words exactly as if he were consulting with Jones . . . about a bitch dog or cow or mare." As Shreve will summarize Sutpen's conversation later: "He suggested that they breed together for test and sample and if it was a boy they would marry." As already indicated, after this conversation Miss Rosa returned to Jefferson, not to see Sutpen's Hundred again for more than forty years. Nearly sixty at the time Rosa left, Sutpen made one last desperate effort to save his design. He seduced Wash Jones's granddaughter, but when she bore him a girl he insulted her—saying to the girl that if she were a mare he could give her a warm stall in the barn. Jones killed Sutpen, his grandchild, and her baby, and was later killed by the sheriff's posse.

These final details of Sutpen's career—the authorial presence breaks his customary pattern of not intruding into his narrative to tell us that most of Rosa's remarks on Sutpen are highly subjective—are lost on Quentin because he can't get beyond "that door" behind which Bon lay. He imagines Henry "with his shaggy bayonet-trimmed hair, his gaunt worn unshaven face, his patched and faded gray tunic, the pistol still hanging against his flank: the two of them, brother and sister curiously alike as if the difference in sex had merely sharpened the common blood to a terrific, and almost unbearable similarity" (AA172). Always active, Quentin's fertile imagination allows him to hear Henry's remark to his sister: "You cannot marry him now because I've killed him."

We have few facts relating the manner in which Quentin spent his time at Harvard during the fall of 1909. Indeed we next see him on a railway siding in Virginia on his way home for Christmas. He gives an old Negro a quarter as a Christmas gift and tells him he'll be back that way "two days after New Years" (SF107). We don't even get the details of Quentin's and Miss Rosa's visit to Sutpen's Hundred until January, 1910, when Shreve and Quentin are discussing a letter from Mr. Compson, in which he relates that Miss Rosa was buried on January 10, after having lain in a coma for two weeks. Knowing Quentin's highly emotional state, however, we can well imagine that during that fall he might have done considerable

94

brooding over what happened to the Sutpen family and why. In fact some of the highly suggestive conclusions he urges on Shreve regarding the strange behavior of the Sutpens suggest that by January, 1910, he has already arrived at solutions to some of that family's problems that are considerably different from those which Mr. Compson had offered. A young man who is utterly confused about his feelings toward his own sister must have found Mr. Compson's speculations about the Bon-Judith-Henry triangle very provocative indeed. For example there is Mr. Compson's attempt to understand the precise nature of the Judith-Bon relationship: "You see? there they are: this girl . . . who sees a man for an average of one hour a day for twelve days during his life and that over a period of a year and a half, yet is bent on marrying him to the extent of forcing her brother to the last resort of homicide" (AA99). Mr. Compson can no more understand this relationship than Quentin can those Caddy had with Dalton Ames and her other lovers. "Did you love them?" Quentin asked her. "When they touched me," she replied, "I died." Mr. Compson can only offer an explanation which he himself would not accept from Quentin. He would not believe Quentin had had an incestuous affair with Caddy; yet he says, "It was Henry who seduced Judith, not Bon." We know, of course, that Mr. Compson is not speaking literally in his reference to Judith and Henry, but in his highly distraught emotional state Quentin cannot be expected to make the necessary figurative leap. Later, as we know, he does confuse Gerald Bland, an acquaintance at Harvard, and Dalton Ames, Caddy's lover.

Mr. Compson's comments about Judith and Henry sound remarkably similar to those he makes in his discussion with Quentin regarding Caddy's promiscuity. To Quentin, referring to Caddy, he says: "it was men invented virginity . . . . women are so delicate so mysterious. . . . Delicate equilibrium of periodical filth between two moons balanced . . . . People . . . cannot do anything very dreadful at all they cannot even remember tomorrow what seemed dreadful today" (SF96). Referring to Henry's attitude toward Judith, he says: Henry may have known "that his fierce provincial's pride in his sister's virginity was a false quality which must incorporate in itself an inability to endure in order to be precious, to exist, and so much depend upon its loss, absence, to have existed at all. In fact, perhaps this is the pure and perfect incest: the brother realizing that the sister's virginity must be destroyed in order to have existed at all, taking that virginity in the person of the brother-in-law, the man he would be if he could become, metamorphose into, the lover, the husband" (AA96).

Quentin and Shreve are motivated by Mr. Compson's letter announcing Rosa's death to attempt to flesh out the skeleton of the Sutpen legend that they know. Shreve is having to do the job with less than Quentin's complete participation because Quentin still cannot pass the door where Judith was standing when Henry came to tell her that he had killed Charles Bon. His mind is filled with an image of "the brother and sister slashing at each other with twelve or fourteen words and most of these the same words repeated two or three times so that when you boiled it down they did it with eight or ten." Quentin's fatally wounded psyche is totally involved in the story of the Sutpen children because it includes both parts of his divided self. In his confused emotional state—one in which he cannot define exactly his feelings toward his sister Caddy—he is attracted to Charles Bon, the brother-seducer. And living always with the knowledge of his shameful behavior when he attempted to defend the family's honor by confronting Dalton Ames on the bridge, he must find much to admire in Henry Sutpen, the brother-avenger. In his attempt to bring his sister's seducer to justice, Quentin has been completely humiliated. First Dalton Ames intercepted the blows which Quentin had aimed at his chin—he had held both of Quentin's hands in one of his—

then Quentin fainted, and Dalton had lied to him and Caddy, saying he had struck Quentin, in order to help Quentin save face. Surely Quentin's interest in the Sutpen family is partially motivated by his subconscious search for self-respect.

In this mood, then, Quentin tells Shreve on that cold January night in Cambridge, Massachusetts, of his visit to the Sutpen home the previous September and of how he had met Henry Sutpen, who had come home to die. Shreve and Quentin consider Mr. Compson's account of Miss Rosa's visit to the old plantation with an ambulance to bring Henry into town for medical attention. They are aware, too, that Clytie has mistaken the purpose of this visit, thinking the sheriff is coming for Henry; therefore she has set fire to the decayed old house, she and Henry perishing in the flames. The only thing left, then, of Sutpen's design is an idiot black boy "to lurk around those ashes and those four gutted chimneys and howl" until someone comes and drives him away.

Together Shreve and Quentin—Faulkner says it might have been either of them speaking and was in a sense both—try to supply some of the missing details in the Sutpen story and to give rational explanations for some of the actions that seem on the surface inexplicable. Quentin's interest in the Judith-Charles-Henry triangle has already been referred to and Shreve apparently would like to tie up some of the loose ends of a fabulous legend that could have occurred only in that faraway Southland that never existed anywhere at anytime except in his imagination. His view of art is that of the classicist; he is seeking artistic unity, to make all of the details fit a preconceived pattern. Among the many missing details that he and Quentin supply through pure speculation are: that Sutpen told Henry that Charles was his brother but that Charles was not aware of this fact; that there was a lawyer in New Orleans maneuvering events so that Charles went to school at the University of Mississippi in order to meet Henry and through him,

Sutpen; that the lawyer wrote Henry, Henry showed the letter to Bon, and Bon guessed that they were brothers; that Charles merely wanted a hint of recognition from his father; that Henry wrestled with the problem of incest and asked Bon "must you marry our sister?"; that Sutpen told Henry that Charles Bon's mother was part Negro.

This last point is a very important one. In spite of the arguments by Olga Vickery, Cleanth Brooks, and others, there is nowhere in the novel convincing evidence that Bon was part Negro. As Ellen Shoenberg has suggested, the conviction that Charles Bon is part Negro is based on the belief that if this supposition were true it would logically explain why Sutpen put aside his first wife. A southern white man wanting to be an aristocratic planter in the 1830s would know that a woman of mixed blood could not possibly fit into his "design." But as reasonable as this explanation for Sutpen's action is, the truth of the mattter is that this supposition usually accepted as truth was created in Quentin's imagination. If indeed it is a fact, it is one that only Quentin knows, and there is no place he could have learned it—not from his father because his father does not know it; not from his grandfather because there is no evidence that Quentin ever spoke to his grandfather about the Sutpen family; not from Henry Sutpen because, despite Cleanth Brooks's insistence, it is highly unlikely that Quentin's one brief meeting with Henry occurred under conditions that would have made the passing of such information possible. One can only conclude that this bit of crucial information came from the disturbed imagination of Quentin Compson, and the inevitable question, therefore, is why?

In his confused state—one, as I have already said, in which he is both Charles Bon and Henry Sutpen—he can well understand the Charles Bon side of his personality. Unable to understand his own feeling toward his sister—his apparent impotence will not allow him to know for certain the nature of his love for

Caddy—he can easily entertain the possibility that one might want to marry his own sister. But why would he kill a brother whom he loves more than anyone else in the world, except to protect the honor of this beloved sister?

To put this matter in proper perspective, one should look again at the famous branch scene of *The Sound and the Fury*. In this, perhaps the central episode in the novel, Caddy wet her dress playing in the branch, and Versh, a young Negro boy a few years older than Caddy, says, "Your mommer going to whip you for getting your dress wet." Caddy replies, "She's not going to do any such thing." And in the ensuing argument, she says she will pull her dress off and let it dry. Quentin tells her she had better not; "You just take your dress off," he warns her. Caddy makes Versh unbutton the dress and she draws it over her head and throws it on the bank to dry, leaving her wearing only her "bodice and drawers." Quentin is so infuriated that Caddy has exposed her body to Versh, a black man, that he "slapped her and she fell down in the water."

Shreve is closer than he knows to expressing Quentin's deepest concerns, therefore, when he says that maybe one day in the spring following the Christmas visit Bon merely concluded, "All right I want to go to bed with a girl who might be my sister." After the four years in the war have settled nothing, Bon must have decided, Shreve and Quentin conclude, definitely to go back and marry Judith. In a scene much like that with Dalton Ames at the bridge—and one created by Quentin's disturbed imagination—Charles hands Henry a pistol and tells him to shoot him if he wishes to prevent the wedding. In Quentin's version Henry is as inept as he was himself at the bridge; Henry's hand trembles as he looks at the pistol: "You are my brother," he says. "No, I'm not," Bon responds, "I'm the nigger that's going to sleep with your sister. Unless you stop me." This remarks arouses Henry. In terms of Quentin's own psychic dilemma, the part of him that is the brother-seducer (Charles

99

Bon) is opposed by the part that is the brother-avenger (Henry Sutpen). In the tale he is concocting, Quentin is able at one stroke to chastise the sister who would expose herself to a black man and to bring to justice the man who would despoil that sister. This remark—"I'm the nigger that's going to sleep with your sister"—provokes immediate action: The boys propose that Henry grabs the pistol from Bon, flings it away, grabs Bon by the shoulder and says, "You shall not! You shall not! Do you hear me?" Bon responds, "You will have to stop me Henry"; and they begin the long ride back to Sutpen's Hundred. When they arrive at the gate and Charles still has not changed his mind, Quentin imagines Henry, with his pistol lying unaimed across his saddle bow, saying: *Don't you pass the shadow of this post.*" (Quentin's ultimatum to Dalton Ames: "Be out of town before sundown.") When Bon passes the shadow, Henry, as Wash Jones says, shoots him "dead as a beef." Then the boy who cannot bear to see his sister strip before their black companion imagines Henry rushing up to his sister, who is threatened with ravishment by a Negro, yelling, "You can't marry him now because I killed him!"

To comprehend the harrowing tale Quentin and Shreve have created out of the sparse set of facts at their disposal, one must always be mindful of Shreve's lack of knowledge of the South. To him it is a not-quite-real kind of place, one in which the fantastic, Gothic legend he and Quentin have concocted could have and probably did occur. But for Quentin the tale is of another quality and serves a different function. A highly disturbed, psychotic personality desperately seeking a solution to the psychic dilemma that threatens to strangle him, he is, I repeat, mentally ill, and like all persons similarly affected, he cannot escape his own set of mental facts. Quentin can relate to Henry Sutpen, however, because Henry is able to avenge a great wrong that threatens his sister. We must realize, however, that the Henry Sutpen of fact, the one who lived near

Jefferson and attended the University of Mississippi, is not the Henry Sutpen that Quentin has created. The real Henry Sutpen undoubtedly was able to place in proper perspective and accept, therefore, an escalating series of Old South taboos: bigamy, bigotry, miscegenation, and maybe even incest. He is sane, if somewhat naïve, and is consequently intensely affected by the attitudes of his society. Quentin, on the other hand, is deeply disturbed and therefore is not rational. Because of the ambiguous nature of his own feeling toward Caddy, he can understand why a man might have erotic desires for his own sister. In his disturbed state, however, he associates promiscuity with miscegenation, which to many in the Old South was promiscuity carried to its most horrible extreme. To fulfill his deepest need, therefore, Quentin creates a Henry who is able to tolerate Bon's marrying his own sister but who is unable to accept the overt promiscuity of a black man sleeping with that beloved sister.

Shreve has fashioned a tale with enough suspense and melodrama to do justice to his conception of the South, a land in which as he expressed it, "it takes two niggers to get rid of one Sutpen." And in the fullness of time he says the Jim Bonds "are going to conquer the western hemisphere." Quentin is not listening too closely, for his interest is not really in Jim Bond, except maybe as his irrational howling reminds him of the sound his brother Benjy makes. When Shreve asks, however, "Why do you hate the South?" Quentin responds in utter frustration, "I don't hate it! I don't hate it! I don't hate it!" For the story Quentin creates and assists Shreve in articulating is only indirectly about the South, and he thinks Shreve has missed the point of his tale. What Quentin is really trying to sort out is precisely how he feels about his sister Caddy and what kind of response his confused emotional state will permit him to make. His is a tale born of desperation. Perhaps his opportunity to create a story detailing the circumstances under which an in-

cestuous love of brother for sister is at least quasi-acceptable—
and at the same time to create his alter ego, a character powerful enough to punish his sister's would-be seducer—provides
Quentin strength to get through the last torturous year of his
life. We see him only twice more: in April, when he returns to
Jefferson to attend Caddy's wedding (when he is a rather as-
sertive, effective young man, getting T. P. and Benjy, who have
had too much champagne, out of the front yard and into the
barn); and on June 2 as he executes a careful, meticulously pre-
pared plan for his own death by leaping from a bridge much
like the one upon which he had humiliated himself before Dalton Ames. His vicarious experience as hero, apparently, could
sustain him no longer.

# The Montage Element
# in Faulkner's Fiction

BRUCE KAWIN

The relations between literature and film are notoriously difficult to sort out. Writing goes back more than four thousand
years, film less than eighty-five; some of the greatest literature
of the twentieth century is regularly characterized as elitist
and noncommercial, just as film is dismissed as populist and
commercial; a book tends to be written by one person in solitude, and a feature film to be made by approximately one hundred people under factory conditions; a word unites a sound and
a concept, while an image unites reflected light and an object.
On the other hand, it is readily apparent that these media have
often told similar stories and engaged in similar meditations;
there is not that much difference between *U.S.A.* and *The Man
with a Movie Camera*, between *Absalom, Absalom!* and *Citizen
Kane*, between *Mutiny on the Bounty* and *Red River*, between
*McTeague* and *Greed*, between *Song of Myself* and *Dog Star
Man*, or even between *Gone with the Wind* and *Gone with the
Wind*. Gertrude Stein insisted, in "Portraits and Repetition,"
that she was "doing what the cinema was doing," even though
she admitted she rarely went to movies and at the time of her
major experiments might not even have seen *any* films. Pound
and Eisenstein, working independently of each other, each recognized their central aesthetic principles in the same source,
the structure of the ideogram, and the montage principle at
work in *The Cantos* is certainly comparable to that in Eisen-

stein's great film *October*. Dos Passos admitted taking inspiration from Eisenstein, and Eisenstein and Ruttmann were the two directors Joyce considered capable of filming *Ulysses*. And although it is often observed that D. W. Griffith took most of his inspiration from Belasco and Dickens rather than from, say, Picasso and Hegel, it is still evident that his *Intolerance*, with its four plots butted together, is a major influence on Russian theories of montage and one of the most accessible prototypes of modernist film. The closer one comes to the present, the more difficult it becomes to discuss the achievements of the most significant films without some appeal to their parallels in modern literature, not just in the extreme example of Alain Robbe-Grillet, but also in the cases of Godard, Resnais, Antonioni, Kubrick, Losey, Fassbinder, Bergman, and Welles. By the same token, it is profligate to consider *Gravity's Rainbow* apart from the work of Fritz Lang, Robert Wiene, and Mack Sennett, not to mention *King Kong* and *The Wizard of Oz*—but one could go further and assert that the two metaphysics central to that novel are those of psychic contact and of film itself. Joyce's interest in silent comedy is reflected in Beckett's *Waiting for Godot*, and Beckett's own reading of what has to be called the metaphysic of Buster Keaton is, as Beckett and Schneider's *Film* incarnates it, a profoundly accurate one, and a good measure of the distance between the contemporary situation, where literature and film can be said to have caught up with each other and to enjoy each other's company, and the twenties, when the author of *The Waste Land* (a montage if ever there was one) could dismiss cinema as a "cheap" and pointless art, and the author of *A la recherche du temps perdu* could wax eloquent on the magic lantern but denigrate both photography and film, considering them incapable of metaphor at the very time his compatriot, Abel Gance, was finishing *La Roue* (which, with *Intolerance*, was one of the two films most carefully studied during the next three years by the Soviets).

And at the center of this vortex spins the complex and brilliant career of William Faulkner, whom I have called the most cinematic of novelists and who considered much of his Hollywood career a terrible waste of time.

One of the most interesting things about the early twentieth century is that the arts of literature, painting, and film went through the modernist crisis at approximately the same time, despite the fact that film was a fledgling art and the others were well into their maturity. Whether they did so in response to each other (influence), or independently, in response to the state of Western culture (parallel development), is extremely difficult to establish. André Bazin has eloquently suggested that novelists have been influenced not by the specific films made in their times but by the *idea* of cinema: "If we maintain that the cinema influences the novel then we must suppose that it is a question of a potential image, existing exclusively behind the magnifying glass of the critic and seen only from where he sits. We would then be talking about the influence of a nonexistent cinema, an ideal cinema, a cinema that the novelist would produce if he were a filmmaker; of an imaginary art that we are still awaiting."[1] It is my contention that this ideal cinema is reflected in the greatest novels and stories of Faulkner but only pops up occasionally in the films he helped to write—that Faulkner at his best was thinking not in terms of movies but in tropes that are most convincingly explicated in cinematic terms. This is to employ the term "cinematic" in an idealized fashion, to say that it appeals to an archetype of kinetic and visual presentation. It is also to be sensitive to the pervasive nature of modernist aesthetics in the crucial works of this century, an aesthetic whose fundamental expression is found in what Eisenstein called the montage trope. The fact that Faulkner the novelist, when he *was* a filmmaker, did not

1. André Bazin, "In Defense of Mixed Cinema," *What Is Cinema?* (Berkeley: University of California Press, 1967), I, 63.

produce "pure cinema" is attributable to a number of factors, ranging from the economics of the film industry and Faulkner's own need for Hollywood money, to the aesthetic convictions of his mentor, Howard Hawks, and Faulkner's own apparent lack of conviction that film was a major art. We can suggest that Faulkner missed the point of some of his own best work, but we can also observe that the montage archetype was pervasive in the culture even apart from the forms it took in various films.

The central anxiety of modernism—that the old, harmonious world lay busted into fragments—was central to its triumph. That triumph consisted in acknowledging fragmentation and then butting the fragments up against each other; this juxtaposition itself did not so much provide the longed-for connective tissue as it pointed beyond itself to a conceptual space in which the fragments might cohere. For instance: we live in a fallen world where archetypal heroes are hard to come by. Joyce gives us Leopold Bloom, who is both parody and the real thing. The reader of *Ulysses* constructs the ultimate Bloom, a "hero" in the modern world, out of two terms—the given Bloom and the implicit Odysseus—whose relationship is purely dialectical. Thesis Bloom evokes antithesis Odysseus; this collision dominates the reader's experience and leads him to generate a synthesis. We could call that synthesis "modern hero" or "Bloom as Odysseus," but it is more proper to call it *Ulysses*. Pound generates an epic history out of fragments of letters, poems, etc., not by trying to include in his poem the continuity they suggest but by letting their juxtaposition speak for itself, so that "the live tradition" truly hovers in "the air" above the poem. This dialectical, fallen space made Eliot nervous and Pound excited; Eliot's nostalgia for the ultimate connection must have had a great deal to do with his conversion, but it was especially significant for its charging *The Waste Land* with the latent instruction, Transcend this fragmentation.

Picasso and Braque fragmented vision into multiple but simultaneous perspectives, past which one had to appeal for a sense not of the object that might have preceded the Cubist painting (the "What *is* that, anyway?" syndrome) but of the object perceived in time and in multiplied space. The basic metaphysic of Proust's *A la recherche du temps perdu* is that Self A, in the present, collides with Self B, from the past; in the instant that they become simultaneous, two things happen: time is abolished, and the timeless Self C becomes manifest yet remains ineffable, unnamable. This is Hegelian dialectics at its most profound and straightforward level: thesis collides with antithesis and generates synthesis. The fact that Proust could not see this same device at work in film is not the point; the point is that it is (in ideal terms) the same device, as becomes clear when one confronts the films and theoretical writings of Eisenstein.

Here are Pound and Eisenstein, each writing somewhat after the fact, on the nature of the ideogram, which is a montage signifier; all they had gone on to do was to add the element of time (the line of words, the ribbon of frames). First Pound, in 1934:

But when the Chinaman wanted to make a picture of something more complicated, or of a general idea, how did he go about it?

He is to define red. How can he do it in a picture that isn't painted in red paint?

He puts (or his ancestors put) together the abbreviated pictures of

ROSE      CHERRY

IRON RUST    FLAMINGO[2]

Now Eisenstein, in 1929:

The point is that the . . . combination of two hieroglyphics of the simplest series is to be regarded not as their sum, but as their prod-

2. Ezra Pound, *ABC of Reading* (New York: New Directions, 1960), 21–22.

uct, i.e., as a value of another dimension, another degree; each, separately, corresponds to an *object*, to a fact, but their combination corresponds to a *concept*. From separate hieroglyphs has been fused —the ideogram. By the combination of two "depictables" is achieved the representation of something that is graphically undepictable.

For example: the picture for water and the picture of an eye signifies "to weep"; the picture of an ear near the drawing of a door = "to listen";

a dog + a mouth = "to bark";

a mouth + a child = "to scream";

a mouth + a bird = "to sing";

a knife + a heart = "sorrow," and so on.

But this is—montage![3]

Montage is the French term for editing or cutting; its sense is that shot A is "mounted" next to shot B, etc. I am using it here in the sense Eisenstein does, concentrating on the special case of "dialectical montage," which means simply that shot A collides with shot B to generate C, a concept in the mind of the viewer. This trope is useful because it is probably impossible to photograph an idea (literature has the edge here), but it is also useful when one is trying to deal with a fragmented world and can't simply name, even with words, the integrating force. And if you accept the Hindu notion that the universe is One and that language—because it splits the truth up into individual words—is hopelessly false, montage is even more useful, even urgent, since it continually calls attention to the need to transcend fragmentation; nor is film, which fragments the world into shots—and angles of view—exempt from the problem. In my book *Telling It Again and Again* (Cornell, 1972) I attempted to show that this problem is relevant whether or not

3. Sergei Eisenstein, "The Cinematographic Principle and the Ideogram," *Film Form* (New York: Harcourt Brace and World, 1949), 29–30. Abel Gance made a similar observation about the hieroglyph; see Walter Benjamin, "The Work of Art in the Age of Mechanical Reproduction," *Illuminations* (New York: Schocken, 1969), 227.

one is a mystic (let alone a modernist) and that the two most interesting tropes for confronting it are montage and repetition, the latter because it is a minimal syntax that charms the mind into a perception of the One. Without going headlong into that argument here I would like to point out that repetition and montage are the two central linguistic and structural devices in Faulkner's fiction, as they are also central to the metaphysics of Proust. To one side of this pair are Pound and Joyce, who were interested more in montage than in repetition, and to the other side are Beckett and Gertrude Stein, to whom repetition was simply basic. I suggest that these six are the most exciting and significant writers of the century, and that this is the way their achievements interrelate.

I hope I have made it clear by now that if I say Faulkner uses montage I mean not that he got the idea from films and not that he thought in terms of films, but that he was doing something that the cinema also did. (His most likely source was Joyce, though he was in fact aware of both Griffith and Eisenstein, each of whom is more relevant to this aspect of film aesthetics than is Hawks.) Let us go on, then, to examine the varieties of montage in his work.

These varieties of montage take five basic and sometimes overlapping forms: the oxymoron, dynamic unresolution, parallel plotting, rapid shifts in time and space, and multiple narration. There is a related aspect of his work, which is the role of photographic imagery, and that may be the best place to start. In the first section of his story "All the Dead Pilots," Faulkner discusses "the snapshots hurriedly made" of the World War I pilots with whom his story is concerned. He suggests that the eye of the writer or of history itself can behave like a flash camera, and also that the snapshot as a form is like an illuminated moment, an incredible concentration of force on the instant:

In the pictures, the snapshots hurriedly made, a little faded, a little

109

dog-eared with the thirteen years, they swagger a little. Lean, hard, in their brass-and-leather martial harness, posed standing beside or leaning upon the esoteric shapes of wire and wood and canvas in which they flew without parachutes, they too have an esoteric look; a look not exactly human, like that of some dim and threatful apotheosis of the race seen for an instant in the glare of a thunderclap and then forever gone.

Faulkner goes on to say that he will take such moments—revelations that are like photographs, the Kodak as epiphany —and arrange them in what one has to call a montage, though he calls it a composite series: "That's why this story is composite: a series of brief glares in which, instantaneous and without depth or perspective, there stood into sight the portent and the threat of what the race could bear and become, in an instant between dark and dark."[4] He is making of his insight a principle of composition. The basic difference between this method and that of *The Sound and the Fury* is that in the latter he mounts together fragmented scenes without having to consider them "without depth or perspective"[5]—that he moves, in other words, from the series of vignettes to the more complex collision of scenes.

Walter Slatoff has shown in *Quest for Failure* that the basic quality of Faulkner's imagination is its ability to suspend oppositions—that his novels build not to resolutions but to the tension of unresolution. If you don't understand this, you run the risk of missing the points of his novels by trying to make everything fit, as in those inane oversimplifications of *As I Lay Dying*, for instance, that convert it into some kind of good-

---

4. *Collected Stories* (New York: Random House, 1950), 511–12.

5. Photography, for Faulkner, was as "flat" as Popeye's stamped-tin face; epiphanic or not, it was characteristically and phenomenologically modern, whereas fiction could achieve a sense of depth from which Faulkner felt less alienated. Even without raising the question of his ignorance of film history, then, it should not be surprising that he did not compare his novels to movies in spite of their structural complementarity.

humored epic of survival, and ignore all that business about language, madness, ruin, and failure, along with what I feel must be called the metaphysical implications of the montage structure of its narrative. To take a simpler example, however, it is important to notice that the last phrase of *The Sound and the Fury*—"each in its ordered place"—has a dialectical relationship with the title and drift of the novel, rendering this sense of order as ironic as possible. The order achieved at the end is created by Jason and through violence; it is artificial, even if the order becomes that of "post and tree" under the serene gaze of the idiot Benjy. The novel's title, of course, implies that the "tale told by an idiot" will be full of sound and fury and might signify nothing; but one must remember that Faulkner is alluding to what Macbeth says when he sees the ruin of his enterprise and just before "the time is [set] free" by his death. (Part of Shakespeare's point is that insane and unnatural control stops time.) One of the characteristics of Faulkner's novel is that time is approached as an organic chaos that could be called "free," at least in that part of the tale that *is* told by the idiot. (Quentin, who is aware of time, has other problems, including a nostalgia for timelessness; the freed time he envisions is that of the Christ who is through with his body so that he is no longer "worn away by a minute clicking of little wheels," but it is also the freedom *in* time characteristic of Benjy and achieved by Quentin whenever he forgets about his watch.) The innocence of Benjy's perceptions is certainly preferable to the rigidity of Jason's. In fact the whole novel is structured between the poles of freedom and control, which represent two kinds of order, the former natural and the latter cultural. Each of the Compson brothers wants to control Caddy, who wants to be free; it is interesting to note that Caddy's being damned and doomed is the result not of her being evil but of her attempt to function as a sexual being, whereas precisely the opposite is true of the more profoundly irresponsible

111

Temple Drake. Caddy's problem is that she is surrounded by controlling forces who will destroy her but whom she loves. The rage to create an artificial order is what drives both the Compson family and Thomas Sutpen, and in both cases it is poor Quentin, the heir of Stephen Dedalus, who is left to puzzle out the cultural shambles but who would really rather live in some paradise before the fall into time and history. Such polar oppositions abound in Faulkner's work, but the simplest way to organize them, in terms of *The Sound and the Fury*, is to say first that the novel begins in apparent disorder and ends in apparent order, and second that the novel begins in an innocence of perception that reveals truth and ends in a sophisticated, third-person perspective that misses a great deal. The sound and fury of the idiot's tale signify most, and it can hardly be an accident that the structure of Benjy's monologue is mirrored in the structure of the novel whose four parts are out of chronological sequence. To strive for order in the manner of the Compson brothers is to achieve the order of death; thus the novel comes to a very dubious sense of rest at its close. Nor should this surprise us, since it is implicit in Quentin's chapter that Easter, whether as historical incident or as the metaphor of the final chapter, didn't solve very much. Similarly, the ending of *Absalom, Absalom!* occurs at a moment of absolute tension; Shreve's attempt to wrap it all up into a flip kind of order ("So it takes two niggers to get rid of one Sutpen") is hardly a resolution, and Quentin's frantic "*I dont hate it!*"—i.e., "I don't want to admit that I hate it"—is the simultaneous X and not-X of unresolution.

If Faulkner thinks in terms of opposites and throws those opposites together, it should be no surprise that one of his central devices is dialectical montage. In a work like *The Wild Palms* he lets these polar perspectives alternate, in the equivalent of a trope that Eisenstein called parallel montage; at the ends of *The Sound and the Fury* and *Absalom, Absalom!* he compresses the opposites into simultaneity—which is not at all to say that he unites them in one term. In this context, there *is* no such term. The oxymoron (a rhetorical device characterized by the juxtaposition of incongruous or contradictory terms) allows him to carry on dialectical montage within the sentence, and is often his way of evoking—through a state of contradiction—that kind of synthesis-term whose equivalent Eisenstein called "graphically undepictable." Here is a representative excerpt from the second page of *Absalom, Absalom!*:

Out of quiet thunderclap he would abrupt (man-horse-demon) upon a scene peaceful and decorous as a schoolprize water color, faint sulphur-reek still in hair clothes and beard, with grouped behind him his band of wild niggers like beasts half tamed to walk upright like men, in attitudes wild and reposed, and manacled among them the French architect with his air grim, haggard, and tatter-ran. Immobile, bearded and hand palm-lifted the horseman sat; behind him the wild blacks and the captive architect huddled quietly, carrying in bloodless paradox the shovels and picks and axes of peaceful conquest. Then in the long unamaze Quentin seemed to watch them overrun suddenly the hundred square miles of tranquil and astonished earth and drag house and formal gardens violently out of the soundless Nothing and clap them down like cards upon a table beneath the up-palm immobile and pontific, creating the Sutpen's Hundred, the *Be Sutpen's Hundred* like the oldentime *Be Light*. Then hearing would reconcile and he would seem to listen to two separate Quentins now.[6]

It is not impossible to imagine a "quiet thunderclap," an attitude "wild and reposed," a shovel in the role of a rifle, a "peaceful conquest," an earth that could be at once "tranquil and astonished," a silent but violent construction project (even if the silence is that of Quentin's mind's eye), and so on. It is not impossible, but the effort involves dialectics, creates a conceptual space in which an event or pose can best be described

6. *Absalom, Absalom!* (New York: Random House, 1936), 8–9.

in terms of the poles it transcends and conjoins. This series of oxymorons leads directly and naturally into the description of Quentin's being split into two selves, and it is of course appropriate to find "the two separate Quentins now talking to one another in the long silence of notpeople, in notlanguage." The oxymoron, in other words, operates within the sentence in the same way that dynamic unresolution structures the novels, and both of these are montage tropes.

Many of Faulkner's doubling gestures that appear simply to be repetitive turn out also to be polar—the two trials at the end of *Sanctuary,* for instance, in each of which the jury is out for the same eight minutes. Each jury finds the innocent defendant to be guilty. But the first jury—Lee Goodwin's—achieves injustice, while the second—Popeye's—achieves legal injustice but poetic justice. It is a process I like to call "repetition in reverse," as if the trials were, in part, mirror-images of each other; in any case, the point is that this is the very edge of the interrelation between repetition and montage, where both are going on and are doing so with the same terms. Two plus two is four (repetition); two times two is four (montage). We still get to "four," but feel different along the way. Something very like this parallel-trial device goes on in the larger structures of the novel, where the innocent Benbow and the innocent Temple are each made to confront the absolute death of innocence, the absolute absence of sanctuary—i.e., of a safe and honorable space to which to retreat from evil and horror (in Temple's case, the corncrib and the class system; in Horace's, the court and the ideal of womanhood). Horace and Temple are—in several crucial respects but not in their entirety—opposites maintained in parallel, like Hamlet and Laertes, or Hamlet and Stephen Dedalus. The device is called parallel montage, and it reaches its most complex and beautiful expression in *The Wild Palms.*

Montage in Faulkner's work is not something added after the fact, not the product of rearrangement, but integral to each fragment. Faulkner did not write the novella "Old Man" and then the novella "Wild Palms" but wrote them in alternation, chapter by chapter, letting each suggest the other. Faulkner used the terms "antithesis" and "counterpoint" to describe the ways these stories gave each other "emphasis."[7] As usual, he appears to have been "doing what the cinema was doing" but thinking in other terms—in this case, dialectics and music. Nevertheless, one finds in this novel a direct reference to Eisenstein, and another to Joan Crawford (who had starred in *Today We Live*). These two references suggest the poles of Faulkner's attitude toward film:

"I thought—" Wilbourne began. But he did not say it. They went on; the last glare of the snow faded and now they entered a scene like something out of an Eisenstein Dante. The gallery became a small amphitheatre, branching off in smaller galleries like the spread fingers from a palm, lighted by an incredible extravagance of electricity as though for a festival—an extravagance of dirty bulbs which had, though in inverse ratio, that same air of sham and moribundity which the big, almost barren building labeled *Commissary* in tremendous new letters had—in the light from which still more of the grimed, giant-seeming men in sheep coats and with eyes which had not slept much lately worked with picks and shovels with that same frenzy of the man running behind the loaded tram, with shouts and ejaculations in that tongue which Wilbourne could not understand almost exactly like a college baseball team cheering one another on, while from the smaller galleries which they had not penetrated yet and where still more electric bulbs glared in the dust-laden and icy air came either echoes or the cries of still other men, meaningless and weird, filling the heavy air like blind erratic birds.[8]

In this first passage, "Eisenstein" may simply be a stand-in term for "Russian," but since the novel itself is so deliberately an act of montage, and since the harshly lit and chaotic mine

7. Malcolm Cowley, *The Faulkner-Cowley File* (New York: Viking, 1968), 164.
8. *The Wild Palms* (New York: Random House, 1939), 186–87.

is described in a manner that echoes the early Eisenstein's mise en scène, I consider it safe to assume that Faulkner did not drop the name lightly. (Eisenstein never met Faulkner, though he did meet Joyce. The closest Eisenstein and Faulkner came to meeting, however, makes a story in itself. Each of them worked on the script of *Sutter's Gold*—Eisenstein in 1930 and Faulkner in 1934—when each was, from Hollywood's point of view, an aesthetic outsider; neither of their scripts was used, though Eisenstein's has been published and Faulkner's has a number of connections with *Absalom, Absalom!*, which followed shortly.) It is certainly significant that Faulkner teams Eisenstein's name with that of Dante, though he uses the former only as an adjective; the sense of the reference, in any case, is to a serious artist.

The reference to Hollywood, on the other hand, is both hostile and generalized:

They rode two nights and a day in day coaches and left the snow behind and found buses now, cheaper now, her head tilted back against the machine-made doily, her face in profile against the dark fleeing snow-free countryside and the little lost towns, the neon, the lunch rooms with broad strong Western girls got up out of Hollywood magazines (Hollywood which is no longer in Hollywood but is stippled by a billion feet of burning colored gas across the face of the American earth) to resemble Joan Crawford, asleep or he could not tell.[9]

Although there appears to be no animosity toward the figure of Joan Crawford, there is a great deal of it toward the cultural imperialism of Hollywood. The "silver dream" of film, as it is described in the story "Dry September," is escapist and dangerous; in *Pylon* his metaphor for film distribution is that of contagion, and its echo of the *Wild Palms* passage is close enough to bear quoting here:

9. *Ibid.*, 209.

116

. . . and looking out through the falling snow she saw a kind of ceno-taph, penurious and without majesty or dignity, of forlorn and vic-torious desolation—a bungalow, a tight flimsy mass of stoops and porte-cochères and flat gables and bays not five years old and built in that colored mud-and-chickenwire tradition which California moving picture films have scattered across North America as if the celluloid carried germs.[10]

For Faulkner, then, the film industry was in the disease busi-ness, but Eisenstein was an artist, and one with whose work he appears to have been familiar. It is possible, then, that Faulk-ner recognized a difference between the terms "Hollywood" and "film," although many of his biographers, critics, and col-leagues seem to have missed that particular boat.

*The Wild Palms*, in any case, tells two parallel but opposite stories, in alternation. "Old Man" is the story of a tall convict whose youthful misfortune was to believe what he read in cheap fiction about the easy rewards of banditry; he is, in other words, very much like Don Quixote—even to the extent that he curses, when he has been imprisoned, not the lawmen who caught him but the authors of the pulps who misled him. The convict is accidentally freed from prison during a flood, and spends most of the rest of the story trying to get back to jail; in the meantime, however, he helps a woman give birth and discovers the rewards of working for a living. He rises to the challenge of freedom and autonomy, but when he is re-captured he does not put up any significant resistance, even when his sentence is drastically increased. His last line is "Women shit," his point being that if it had not been for the pregnant flood victim who needed rescuing, the convict might never have really had to deal with life.

Harry Wilbourne's last line, however, as he sits in jail at the end of "Wild Palms," is *"between grief and nothing I will take*

10. *Pylon* (New York: Signet, 1968), 215.

*grief.*" Grief is his memory of his beloved Charlotte, who would cease to exist—along with what is left of their love—if he were, by committing suicide, to cease being able to remember her. Harry is dragged away from his safe life as a medical student by Charlotte, a romantic overreacher who hooks him on the ideal of absolute and realized love—a hook on which he proves to be even more caught than she. The freedom to love completely, however, is almost impossible in society, and even their escape to the wilderness confronts them with both the cultural and the existential limits of their quest. (They are like some Don Quixote who could see what was really going on.) Where the convict helps a woman deliver a child, Harry—who has medical training but is too emotionally involved to do the job correctly and in time—botches Charlotte's abortion and thereby causes her death. At the end, then, Harry and the convict are both in jail. Each has been yanked into freedom by a woman, each has some nostalgia for the safe life before the crisis, and each has been trapped by society's insensitive enforcers. But the convict had found freedom through a kind of passivity (his characteristic pose is to lie on his back and bleed), while Harry had pursued his freedom like a grail. Both the convict and Harry begin in safety, go through a period of activity and growth, and end in a state of arrest—but their perspectives are precisely opposite. It is a definitive example of parallel montage, giving rise to a complex vision of the demands of freedom and the nature of endurance that neither story, on its own, presents.

The term "montage" is more regularly associated, however, not with this elegant device of continuing antithetical counterpoint, but with the more apparently chaotic series of pell-mell collisions achieved through "rapid cutting." The most famous examples of rapid cutting—which was perfected by Abel Gance but had such an influence on the Soviets that it came to be known as "Russian cutting" before the term "montage" subsumed it—are Gance's *La Roue* and *Napoléon*, and Eisenstein's *Potemkin* and *October*. Many of the shots in these films are only two frames—about an eighth of a second—in length. The sense of collision here is more kinetic than intellectual (the dialectical processes are still at work, but the shots go by so rapidly that one tends to miss some of the conceptual overtones, unless one can examine the film on an editing bench). One way to conceptualize the difference in rhythm between parallel montage and rapid cutting is to compare *Intolerance* with the Odessa Steps sequence in *Potemkin*, the alternating narrators of *Bleak House* with those of *As I Lay Dying*, or *The Wild Palms* with *The Sound and the Fury*.

*The Sound and the Fury* is structured by oppositions and characterized by collisions. The cinematic feel of this novel is the result of two challenges Faulkner set himself in the Benjy section but which show up, in simpler terms, in the other three chapters. Because Benjy is an idiot and does not have words for most of the things he encounters, his experience is highly sensual; his dominant sense is the visual. It is clear from how it looks that the opening scene is of golfing, for example, and that Benjy does not know the word (or have the full thought) for that. Benjy's chapter is a sequence of primarily visual scenes, with sound and scent and touch playing important but secondary roles; it is a series of views, transcribed by a writer.

The second challenge was to dramatize psychological time. While most of us can think about our experience through a combination of memory and verbal labeling, Benjy's associative process actually hurtles him from one event to another in a sequence of (re)livings. The reader understands that many of these are memories and that the links among scenes (dialectically generated) are the nearest Benjy comes to thinking: this looks like that, this feels like that. Benjy cannot rise to generalization, cannot interrelate concepts, cannot distinguish past from present—but he can *feel* the difference between scene A, where Caddy is around, and scene B, where she is not, and start to bellow. The reader achieves complex insights from the montage inside Benjy's head; one *watches* Benjy's mental experience and understands the rudiments of human thought (Benjy has subjectivity but not consciousness; "consciousness" is used here in the sense suggested by Ervin Laszlo: "awareness of subjectivity"). Benjy is going through a series of Proustian shifts—nonverbal association as time travel—but cannot step back and watch himself or understand what these shifts mean. This is the closest Proust and Faulkner get to each other, so this is as good a time as any to quote Robbe-Grillet, who considers them two of the basic influences on modern fiction and film:

The cinema knows only one grammatical mode: the present tense of the indicative. In any case, film and novel today meet in the construction of moments, of intervals, and of sequences which no longer have anything to do with those of clocks or calendars. Let us try to specify their role a little.

It has very often been repeated in recent years that time was the chief "character" of the contemporary novel. Since Proust, since Faulkner, the flashback, the break in chronology seem in effect at the basis of the very organization of the narrative, of its architecture. The same is obviously true of the cinema: every modern cinematographic work is a reflection on human memory, its uncertainties, its persistence, its dramas, etc.

All of which is said a little too quickly.[11]

Like film, Benjy's mind has only one tense. (This is, by the way, the key to Gertrude Stein's basic insight about the continuous present in film, literature, repetition, and consciousness.) For Benjy the contents of a memory are present events. It works the same way in film: it is only through context that one understands a given scene as "not happening right now"—

11. Alain Robbe-Grillet, "Time and Description," *For a New Novel* (New York: Grove, 1965), 151–52.

the point being, of course, that it *is* happening right now and only now, and that any other chronology is metatextual. The order of Benjy's scenes *is* his mental experience. By being true to his conception of an idiot's visual, kinetic stream of consciousness, Faulkner developed a narrative mode that really cannot be called anything but cinematic, since it presents the story in a series of visions, both of the mind's eye and of the physical eye, with all narrative time being present and all transitions *de facto*, instantaneous, cuts. A cut is an instantaneous shift in time and space; one is at X, and now one is at Y. Without saying more about it, let me simply quote one of Benjy's associative transitions and ask you to think of this as a three-shot sequence:

We went along the fence and came to the garden fence, where our shadows were. My shadow was higher than Luster's on the fence. We came to the broken place and went through it.

"Wait a minute." Luster said. "You snagged on that nail again. Cant you never crawl through here without snagging on that nail."

*Caddy uncaught me and we crawled through. Uncle Maury said to not let anybody see us, so we better stoop over, Caddy said. Stoop over, Benjy. Like this, see. We stooped over and crossed the garden, where the flowers rasped and rattled against us. The ground was hard. We climbed the fence, where the pigs were grunting and snuffing. I expect they're sorry because one of them got killed today, Caddy said. The ground was hard, churned and knotted.*

*Keep your hands in your pockets, Caddy said. Or they'll get froze. You don't want your hands froze on Christmas, do you.*

"It's too cold out there." Versh said. "You don't want to go out doors."

"What is it now." Mother said.[12]

The tense used throughout Benjy's section is the past. This does *not* signify that Benjy knows the difference between now

12. *The Sound and the Fury* (New York: Random House, 1929 facsimile [n.d.]), 3.

and then, but instead asserts the equivalence of all time, and does so in a tense with which the reader can deal easily (tense is used with greater complexity in *As I Lay Dying*). In any case, the logic of the cuts is clear: Benjy gets caught on the fence while he is with Luster, and flashes to his getting caught on that fence when he was with Caddy. He lives in that other scene, then, as Caddy gets him uncaught; it is Christmas and the ground is frozen. Caddy tells him to keep his hands in his pockets because it's cold, and he cuts to another scene in which Versh had told him something similar. The reader feels the collision and understands the link. Scene follows scene in a chaos that is only apparent and in a syntax that is thoroughly cinematic, not just because it is comparable to dialectical montage and not just because it reminds one of Resnais as much as of Eisenstein, and regardless of whether Faulkner was thinking in terms of film, but primarily because it is told in one tense, with straight cuts, and with minimal appeal to the act of naming things. Benjy thinks like a modernist film, and Faulkner discovered a means of dramatizing that process so that the reader could, in his mind's eye, *see* Benjy's thinking. One could film *The Sound and the Fury* with hardly a change—even Quentin's section, which cuts less frequently but in the same manner as Benjy's (since Faulkner is saying something universal about thought) but is easier to follow, since Quentin knows the names for more things and can conceptualize time. Jason is more rigid, more locked away from fluid phenomena into a wall of preconceptions, but even he has his share of flashbacks. The final section is conventionally chronological and third-person. No matter how eloquent the narrative in that last chapter, then, one is alienated from its capping the novel's increasing sense of order, as if a complex and tasty solution had precipitated itself into a beaker of water and a couple of little rocks. The more conventional the narrative becomes, the more it moves from "ideal cinema" to nineteenth-century narrative, the more its order seems imposed and artificial, cut-off and closed, not just to the film-oriented critic but to anyone who has been paying attention to Jason (whom Faulkner must have been in a very bitter and ironic mood to have characterized as "sane").

In *Absalom, Absalom!*, however, as in much of *As I Lay Dying*, the primary orientation of the narrative is toward language and not toward the visual. The montage here—which builds on that of the four parts of *The Sound and the Fury*—is of narrative points of view, and the conceptual interactions are extraordinary. Even so, one of the first and most arresting things that happens in *Absalom* is that the tensions of language embattled against itself (in dialectics, in oxymorons, in Rosa's voice, in Quentin's character, and so on) result in the *vanishing* of language and the appearance of the figure of Sutpen as an image in Quentin's mind's eye, an inner theater which is, significantly, as silent as the films of his period.

Sutpen is the embodiment of the concept that arises from the collision of attempts to describe him. Sutpen is not *in* the novel, just as Charles Foster Kane is not *in* Welles's film. To be more precise: Kane appears in the narrative present of *Citizen Kane* only in fragments (a close-up of his mouth, a hand, a shadow) and then only at the moment of his death; all the rest of the time one sees only the images of Kane that his friends and associates and the news media have of him, images that reflect each narrator's bias. With the camera—even more than with the reporter, Thompson, who is less than a Quentin figure —the viewer explores the pieces of the puzzle and assembles them into a concept of the hero's nature; the dialectic of points of view impels one to generate a synthesis, Kane, who does not and probably cannot appear whole in the film.

To paraphrase Beckett in *Watt*, the ineffable is what one can't eff. Not just a demon, a madman, a patriarch, an Agamemnon, a David, a Shakespeare, a victim of colonization, and

123

an imperialist, Sutpen is primarily an occasion for meditation—
and a particularly fine one in that he eludes exhaustive description; what he does is to exhaust description. He does this not
because he is some kind of transcendent figure but because the
method of description itself generates the sense of its own failure. That failure generates further attempts, and the rhetoric
and pace of the work become an eloquent frenzy; nailing this
henhouse together in a hurricane, Faulkner achieves something
that is metaphysically startling: the henhouse *as* hurricane.
What is at stake here is not the nature and history of Sutpen
but the indomitability and impotence of language.

When description A fails, and description B fails, one can
hope that their juxtaposition will point toward C, the thing
itself (by which I mean not Sutpen the man but Sutpen the
force or concept). *Absalom* is montage's last stand, the trope
chosen because montage is an important and perhaps necessary means of dealing not just with the "graphically undepictable" but with its linguistic equivalent, the inconceivable. The
problem of the ineffable is one that seems not to have troubled
Joyce, even though Stephen does think about it ("Ineluctable
modality of the visible," etc.); in this context, Joyce's limitation
as an artist is that he had a word for everything, that given infinite time he appears to have felt that he could carve almost
anything out of the not-yet-said. The problem is central, however, to Proust and Faulkner as well as to Beckett (whose ties
with Joyce are, I feel, much overstated; the place to locate
Beckett is between Proust and Stein). The ineffable *per se* does
not play a crucial thematic role in *Absalom* or *Kane*—it is more
a case of by direction finding indirection out—but the dialectical process does, the problem of accurate description is paramount, and the generated concept of the hero exists (or takes
place) outside each work. Where this all comes together is, of
course, in the montage narrative of *As I Lay Dying*, a novel
centrally concerned with the limits of language and of con-

sciousness, whose "I" is either that of the novel or that of a
woman who "speaks" long after she has begun to decompose,
and whose major narrator (Darl)—at the moment he begins to
make contact with the narrative force that arises out of the
montage of individual narrators, to which Addie is ineffably
connected and for which she is perhaps responsible—suffers a
split into two voices, for one of which he is "I" and for the
other "Darl."

Rather than attempt to explicate *As I Lay Dying*, however
—since that would take at least as much time as I have already
taken—I would simply like to suggest that Hegel had a profound intuition when he proposed dialectics as a means by
which the ineffable could realize itself, that Eisenstein incorporated this aspect of dialectics into his own theories when he
suggested that a synthesis could be "graphically undepictable," and that Faulkner often used montage not just for psychological realism, for rhythm, and for conceptual complexity,
but also as a means of turning language against itself so that
such unnamables as the power behind Sutpen's power and the
language of Addie's silence could, in Wittgenstein's highly appropriate phrase, "make themselves manifest."

The connection between *Kane* and *Absalom* raises one final
point. It is difficult, as I've said, to prove Faulkner was influenced by the cinema; on the other hand, it is clear that cinema
has been influenced by Faulkner—not Faulkner the screenwriter, but Faulkner the novelist. *Absalom* came out three years
before Herman J. Mankiewicz wrote the script for *Kane*, and
there is no way to know for certain whether that novel was an
influence on that film, especially since Mankiewicz's widow
has said he was definitely influenced by *The Great Gatsby*; so
one may have a case here of Mankiewicz's and Faulkner's each
discovering the same way of complicating the collision between the antihero and his observers that Fitzgerald explored.
*Kane* itself, however, was a profound influence on the next

125

generation's sense of narrative complexity, effectively readying such directors as Resnais and Fellini to deal with material of Faulknerian intricacy. The catalyst was the translation into French of *The Wild Palms*, which preceded the New Wave by less than five years. Agnès Varda was inspired by that newly translated novel to write and direct a film with two parallel plots, *La Pointe-Courte*, which is generally considered the first New Wave film and which was edited by her friend Resnais. Resnais led Duras and Robbe-Grillet—novelists who were, to say the least, familiar with Faulkner's work—into scripting *Hiroshima, mon amour* and *Last Year at Marienbad*, respectively, and made possible—though not entirely legitimate—Robbe-Grillet's characterization of "every modern cinematographic work" as a dramatization of mental time. For Robbe-Grillet the crucial Faulkner novel is presumably *The Sound and the Fury*, but it is *The Wild Palms* that keeps showing up, even in so recent a work as Wenders's *Kings of the Road*. Godard has adapted *The Wild Palms* three times, in *Breathless*, *Pierrot le fou*, and the great diptych, *Made in U.S.A.* and *2 or 3 Things I Know About Her*. One of the last projects of the transcendent genius Carl Dreyer was to have been an adaptation of *Light in August*. The point, of course, is not that Faulkner's stories are being turned into movies, but that his *methods* are deliberately being used in films and that Faulkner has indirectly kept the art of film in touch with its own modernist heritage as well as enriched the psychological and metaphysical applications of the montage trope. So the "ideal cinema" Faulkner practiced found its way at last into the movie theaters, regardless of whether it started there in the first place, and can now be seen to have had as profound an influence on film as it has had on the history of modern literature.

# The Effect of Painting on Faulkner's Poetic Form*

ILSE DUSOIR LIND

At the time I submitted the title of this presentation many
months ago, I planned to discuss the relationship which exists
between Faulkner's literary style and the painting style of several of the painters whose work he viewed on his visit to Paris
in 1925, especially that of Cézanne, thinking to show, in the
way several critics have done for Hemingway and Gertrude
Stein, how analogies between the visual medium and the literary one may be said to exist. Such an undertaking still seems to
me worthwhile, but as I surveyed Faulkner's entire relation to
the visual arts, it seemed that such a focus was too narrow,
especially at the present stage of our understanding of Faulkner's art interests. For unlike Gertrude Stein and Hemingway,
who were primarily connoisseurs and collectors, Faulkner's involvement with the visual arts was of an active nature—was the
expression of what was actually a multiple creativity. Almost
as early as Faulkner could write stories and poems, he began to
draw and sketch.[1] His cartoons and illustrations, upon which
he lavished much attention between 1914 and 1922, reveal increasing individuality and sophistication of style. Until at least
1921, when he visited New York City with the thought of
studying art, he seriously contemplated a career in that medium.[2] In New Orleans, besides having Sherwood Anderson as a

* Text of a slide lecture.

1. Joseph Blotner, *Faulkner: A Biography* (New York: Random House,
1974), I, 94.
2. *Ibid.*, 315–16.

literary mentor, he had as a mentor in art the brilliant and versatile William Spratling, who painted, taught architecture and art, designed sets for Le Pétit Théâtre in New Orleans, and studied anthropology in preparation for the Mexican sojourn in which he revived the native silver crafts there. Spratling had been to the Beaux Arts in Paris, was thoroughly oriented in French modernism, and was able to direct Faulkner's education in modern painting, recommending that Faulkner read, in preparation for his European sojourn in 1925, Clive Bell's study of the neoimpressionists and Eli Faure's recent *Outlines of the History of Art*.[3]

It is of more than casual significance that Faulkner did not draw or paint after he became a novelist, especially in light of the fact that the era out of which he evolved was one that championed the unity of all the arts. Kokoschka and Strindberg both painted and wrote plays; Herman Hesse, D. H. Lawrence, Sherwood Anderson, and Henry Miller—to name only a few—painted enough to warrant their having individual exhibitions.[4] All viewed creativity as a fountain that could splash in any direction. Faulkner ceased drawing after he wrote *Soldiers' Pay*, though his interest in the visual arts was then at its height, and he was beginning a new novel, the unpublished *Elmer*, about a would-be painter. He was never asked why he ceased, but a guess may be hazarded. One of the risks of developing a dual creativity is the dilution of one of the two aptitudes, the cultivation of an enthusiastic amateurism. To a considerable degree Sherwood Anderson at the time Faulkner

3. William Spratling, *File on Spratling* (Boston: Little, Brown and Co., 1967), 233. The references to Clive Bell and Eli Faure appear in *Elmer* and probably reflect Spratling's influence. In the unpublished novel, Faulkner has his comic protagonist bring these volumes aboard the freighter which he will take to Europe to study painting. See Thomas H. McHaney, "The Elmer Papers: Faulkner's Comic Portrait of the Artist," in James B. Meriwether (ed.), *Faulkner Miscellany* (Jackson: University Press of Mississippi, 1974), 48.

4. Walter Sorrell, *The Duality of Vision: Genius and Versatility in the Arts* (New York: Bobbs Merrill Co., Inc., n.d.), 255–77.

knew him (the post–*Winesburg, Ohio,* Anderson, who was touring the country preaching modernism and inspirationalism) was guilty of this;[5] in any case, this was the aspect of Anderson that Spratling and Faulkner ridiculed in their satire *Sherwood Anderson and Other American Creoles.*

After Faulkner had completed his first novel, it is evident that he chose to subordinate his secondary talent, to place it at the service of his emerging genius as a fiction writer. But how, precisely, did he make it serve him? This question seemed to me, on further reflection, to be the one which most needs addressing. A revised topic for this talk, therefore, might be: "Multiple Creativity: An Exploration"; or, "Faulkner's Secondary Talent: Notes and Observations." My present purpose is to open inquiry into this area, to be suggestive, not definitive.

My plan is to pursue the relationship that exists between Faulkner's fiction and the visual arts along lines that Faulkner's work itself suggests. I shall therefore be noting, in very selective fashion, a variety of different elements. Sometimes I shall be pointing to similarities in the way Faulkner served an artistic and a literary apprenticeship. Sometimes I shall be giving evidence of the way a specific artist like Beardsley exerted an overwhelming influence. Sometimes I shall be suggesting ways in which Faulkner incorporated into his fiction descriptions of specific pictures that support the theme or structure of a given work. Sometimes I shall note the kinds of pictures he especial-

---

5. Sherwood Anderson, *The Modern Writer* (San Francisco: The Lantern Press, 1925); this is the printed version of the lecture which Anderson gave on his cross-country tour. An impression of Anderson at this time is contained in a letter from Lyle Saxon to Noel Strauss (December 31, 1925): "I went down to Sherwood Anderson's for tea yesterday afternoon. . . . He's fat and prosperous looking, with new tweed suits and a gleam in his eye when he tells of his lecture tours. He has cleaned up, rather, especially at college towns, where the students welcome him with open arms and the faculty asks him, privately, not to put notions in the boys' heads. Sherwood loves that, of course." Mss. Archives, Tulane University. For access to Mss. Archives, I wish to thank Tulane University Library.

ly admired, so as to convey a clearer idea of his predilections. Sometimes I shall show analogies between his fiction and the group of painters known as the expressionists. Sometimes I shall note illustrations that call to mind images in Faulkner's fiction. Sometimes—and finally—I shall give evidence that his responsiveness to the visual arts continued throughout his career.

The first two decades of the century were the golden age of cartooning. Faulkner was drawn to it and taught himself by means of imitation—of British cartoonists and of the whimsical satirist John Held, Jr., who depicted jellybeans and flappers and their ways. With a few dazzlingly witty strokes, Held could render a satiric commentary on the customs of the youth of the day. One such cartoon, for example, is a satiric commentary on the bygone institution of necking.[6] Faulkner similarly— and appropriately enough for the college publications in which his work appeared—did humorous commentaries on customs and fashions among coeds, as, for example, on the vogue of abbreviated skirts for women and neck scarves for men. One of his humorous illustrations shows how such garments could create a conflict of interests on a windy day.[7]

Flying captured the imagination of the young in the early twenties. John Held, Jr., in a cartoon showing a flapper making a transatlantic flight, depicts flying as a style rather than as a skill, through the modish manner with which the flapper wears her flying helmet and cuffed leather pilot gloves and the way she waves her hand airily.[8] Faulkner, similarly, drew a humorous airplane illustration, showing a man who is either trying to board or to disembark a biplane by means of one of the rope

6. *The Art of John Held, Jr.*, Exhibition Catalogue, Graham Gallery (New York, October 28–November 22, 1969), 16.

7. Carvel Collins (ed.), *William Faulkner: Early Prose and Poetry* (Boston: Little, Brown and Co., 1962), 66.

8. *The Art of John Held, Jr.*, 3.

ladders which, early in the history of flying, were adapted from marine use to aviation. In Faulkner's drawing, the moving propellers show the plane to be already in motion, leaving the man on the ladder suspended in midair.[9]

Faulkner, while he was at the beginning stages of both drawing and writing, learned by means of imitation, displaying that flypaper quality of mind to which Professor Kenner alluded in his lecture on Faulkner and Joyce. Soon thereafter, however, Faulkner expressed his own individuality, as shown, for example, in the illustration of social activities in the college yearbook, where a couple is depicted as doing the Charleston with pointed coattails flying in such a way as to suggest that more than two feet are in the air.[10] A distinctive feature of Faulkner's illustrations that is clearly in evidence here is the dominance of line and design over realistic detail, so that hands and feet are rendered in almost mannerist fashion.

Faulkner's response to the work of Beardsley was unusually intense. The affinity was based on Faulkner's being attuned to fin-de-siècle attitudes and fin-de-siècle styles, of which Beardsley was a major creator, as well as upon certain personal attitudes which the two shared. Both were young, for example —Beardsley died while still in his mid-twenties—and both were in rebellion against Victorian staidness and prudery. Beardsley was also an incontestably brilliant illustrator, attracting Faulkner by virtue of his sheer genius. *The Yellow Book* faded soon after Beardsley's illustrations ceased to appear there.

Beardsley influenced Faulkner in more than one direction. Faulkner's mature cartoons show the Beardsley influence in the organization of specific cartoons, as shown through comparison of the structure of certain drawings. Beardsley's illustration of *The Scarlet Pastorale*, for example, with its sinister

9. Collins (ed.), *William Faulkner*, 120.
10. *Ibid.*, 69.

131

harlequin figure announcing a masked ball that will turn into a saturnalia,[11] bears a structural resemblance to Faulkner's drawing of a modern Columbine and Pierrot dancing to music provided by a black banjo player.[12] The themes of the two illustrations are different, but the visual elements are organized in a similar manner. The design of Harlequin's trousers in the Beardsley illustration appear in the floor of Faulkner's (as well as, to a lesser degree, in the man's trousers), and in both, the candelabra are symmetrically balanced.

Beardsley and Faulkner each had a fondness for harlequin figures, through which they represented and distanced complex emotions. Beardsley illustrated Dowson's *Pierrot of the Minute*, which showed Pierrot as the naïve clown-lover, with white pantaloons and shirt, white blouse, and white face. This illustration provided the frontispiece of Dowson's volume.[13] Faulkner employed the harlequin clown-lover as a central figure in *Marionettes*. Beardsley illustrated the death of Harlequin, depicting Harlequin in bed, his mask and his costume on a chair, with the troupe of players in costume attending.[14] This dramatic projection is very similar to the acting out of an imagined scene among the commedia dell'arte players which takes place in Faulkner's poem *Fantoches*.

The concept of the faun also appears frequently in Beardsley. In that era the faun expressed delicacy and grace combined with an erotic freedom, a spontaneity of sexual feeling, which Victorian mores did not allow. In Beardsley, the faun invariably also represented the creative artist. In one of Beards-

11. Bruce Harris (ed.), *The Collected Drawings of Aubrey Beardsley* (New York: Crescent Books, Inc., 1967), 89. Beardsley calls this illustration *The Scarlet Pastorale*. For the privilege of using its extensive Beardsley collection, I wish to thank the Princeton University Library.

12. Blotner, *Faulkner*, I, 273.

13. Frontispiece to Dowson, *Pierrot of the Minute, A Dramatic Phantasy in One Act* (London: Leonard Smithers, 1879).

14. Aubrey Beardsley, *Selected Drawings* (New York: Grove Press, 1967), Illustration No. 89.

ley's many bookplates, he utilizes the faun theme, representing the faun in the act of reading to an attractive young woman, whom he seems to be courting.[15] The illustration calls to mind Faulkner's remark about *The Rubáiyát* being essential to the pursuit of certain courtships he carried on while he was an adolescent. Beardsley gave some of his fauns the faces of artists that he knew, like Whistler or Davidson. This reminds us that Faulkner too was personifying an artist—himself—in the figure of the faun in his long poem *The Marble Faun.*

Attention has often been called to Faulkner's description of Margaret Powers in *Soldiers' Pay* as the kind of girl "Beardsley would have sickened after."[16] Through his illustrations for *The Yellow Book*, Beardsley had created the Beardsley girl; her face appears on one of the covers of *The Yellow Book*, providing a clear image of the type of girl Faulkner had in mind.[17] One of her distinguishing features was a large, well-defined mouth, as contrasted to the cupid and rosebud mouths of earlier fashion.[18] When criticized for his representation of this feature, Beardsley maintained that in real life many women had such mouths.

Beardsley's illustrations for Wilde's *Salomé* made, as we know, an indelible impression on Faulkner. In *Light in August*

15. Cover design for *The Yellow Book* Prospectus for Vol. V, 1895. Not used in Vol. V. Printed instead for Smither's *Catalogue of Rare Books*, No. 60.

16. References are to the first edition or to facsimiles of the first edition except where the work is currently available in hardcover Modern Library editions.

17. *The Yellow Book* (London: John Lane, October, 1894), III. Beardsley did many versions of the type, one of the most appealing being Helen in *The Toilet of Helen* in *Under the Hill* (London: John Lane, 1904). Other characteristics of the Beardsley girl are masses of luxurious black hair, a starkly pale face, eyes half-open in an attitude of inward contemplation, a tall body, exquisite in gesture, and a forthrightness of manner which was almost masculine.

18. A. C. Bross, "*Soldiers' Pay* and the Art of Aubrey Beardsley," *American Quarterly*, I (Spring, 1967), 2–23, examines in detail the influence of Beardsley on *Soldiers' Pay* and notes also references to Beardsley which appear in *Light in August* and *Absalom, Absalom!*

Faulkner describes Joanna Burden, during her love affair with Joe Christmas, as maintaining those "formally erotic attitudes and gestures as a Beardsley of the time of Petronius might have drawn" (227). Beardsley's illustrations of Salomé (unlike Moreau's famous painting, which depicts a delicately beautiful young woman dancing before Herod) stresses the morbidity of Salomé's passion. In the concluding scene of Wilde's play, Salomé insists that she will kiss the severed head of John the Baptist. Beardsley's illustration shows her to be depraved, frenzied, ecstatic with a morbid passion.[19] It is significant in Beardsley's illustration that he placed emphasis upon Salomé's head and facial expression, thereby giving representation to her inner state, her psychic diabolism, which he enters into empathetically. Faulkner similarly presents Joanna Burden with understanding, even while emphasizing the extent to which she is psychologically warped. Faulkner extends this kind of empathy also to the diabolically impassioned Emily Grierson in "A Rose for Emily," who sleeps with her lover after she has killed him. Interestingly, in Beardsley's illustration of Salomé before the beheading, he introduces a peacock motif as a symbol of the decadence of Herod's court, which Salomé's actions in some measure express.[20] This motif is important in Faulkner's work as well. In his play *Marionettes* Faulkner introduces peacocks into the set to symbolize artistic decadence. In his illustration, Beardsley also places a butterfly in an area of black, thereby offering a tribute to Whistler, who had evolved and popularized the peacock design in this era and who also used a butterfly—a yellow butterfly—as his personal signature in his paintings. Yellow butterflies appear in *The Sound and the Fury* (151, 152, 175) as part of a motif involving the color yellow, symbolizing decadence.

The strong impression Beardsley made on Faulkner ap-

19. Beardsley, *Selected Drawings*, Illustration No. 14.
20. *Ibid.*, No. 9.

pears also in an illustration by Beardsley which contains the words "*Et in Arcadia Ego.*"[21] There Beardsley presents the Latin quotation appearing in an inscription in a cemetery where a middle-aged man walks meditatively. In Faulkner's *The Sound and the Fury*, Mr. Compson utters the unexpected Latin sentence during one of his conversations with Quentin, adding, "I have forgotten the Latin for hay" (62).

Individual paintings seem to enter into the basic conception of at least two novels. In *Mosquitoes*, the work in which Faulkner dealt with his various ideas about art, a major theme is decadence, as expressed through the heat of the city, which is constantly causing decay, through allusions to the work of decadent writers like Dowson. As this theme is evolved in the novel, the idea is suggested that new life, new art, comes out of rottenness and death. The book ends with a decadent fantasy, so strange that it seems surrealistic, though surrealism as an artistic movement had not fully developed. The odd visual material of this fantasy seems to have been drawn, to a considerable extent, from paintings mentioned in Huysman's *Against the Grain*, the book which was the bible of the esthetes. In that novel the hero, Des Esseintes, who lives to cultivate his senses, spends much of his time in his room, on the wall of which are two pictures: Rudolphe Bresdin's *The Comedy of Death* and Gustave Moreau's *Les Prétendants*. *The Comedy of Death*, a lithograph,[22] had been the frontispiece to Baudelaire's *Fleurs du Mal* and was well known to the decadents and symbolists.[23] It shows a beggar lying down about to die; the figure of death appears nearby. Deathheads are interwoven throughout the entire lithograph in an intricately worked pattern. In Faulk-

21. Beardsley, *The Collected Drawings*, 134. Appeared originally in *The Savoy*, No. 8.

22. J. B. Newman, *Rodolphe Bresdin* (New York: Oeuvre Catalogue, hand-pasted, Museum of Modern Art), Illustration No. 44, 29.

23. Essays in tribute to Bresdin in *The Massachusetts Review*, II (Autumn, 1960), 73–101.

ner's novel, a beggar is shown lying on the ground. "Rats like dull and cunning silver, keen and plump as death steal toward him, dragging their hot bellies over his lean and age-chilled body, sniffing his intimate parts" (336). In Bresdin's lithograph rats are shown approaching the dying beggar, crawling up his legs toward his genitals.

The second picture in Des Esseintes's studio was Moreau's *Les Prétendants*.[24] Moreau had painted the picture of Salomé dancing before Herod, which was a key work for symbolist writers. His painting style was visionary at the same time that it was extremely detailed and precise. *Les Prétendants* shows an inferno-like mélange of lamenting people—a kind of Dantesque inferno of the sort that Sergei Eisenstein might have rendered—as well as other images which parallel in general feeling (and with some correspondences of detail) Faulkner's references to "the young boy daubed in vermillion carrying a crown . . . the headless naked body of a woman carved of ebony, surrounded by women wearing skins of slain beasts and chained to one another lamenting," and the "fading placidity of the ungirdled maiden," which are mentioned in the phantasmagoria at the end of *Mosquitoes* (337–38). Both Bresdin and Moreau as artists tended to overcrowd their visionary worlds, an impulse also characteristic of Faulkner. In *Mosquitoes* Faulkner seems to be saying through the visionary material that his concept of art includes, in Baudelairean fashion, acceptance of death and evil as fundamental aspects of human life.

Among the neomoderns another painter beloved of the French symbolists—one who identified personally with them in

24. Musée Gustave Moreau, Paris. Ragnar Von Holton, *L'Art Fantastique de Gustave Moreau* (Paris: Jean-Jacques Pauvert Editeur, 1960). Detail, Eulyssé et le jeun homme mourant, Plate IV, p. 37. Entire painting, Illustration 69, 69–70. For an account of Moreau's extraordinary significance for symbolists, see Julius Kaplan, *Gustave Moreau* (Los Angeles: Los Angeles County Museum of Art and New York Graphic Society, 1974), 10–35.

their literary causes—was Paul Gauguin. Especially admired were his canvases of bright color and strong design, with suppression of depth. After Gauguin went to Tahiti, he completed what was in effect a triptych of the Passion with *Nativity*,[25] which shows a native girl who had borne him a child. Lying in her hut shortly after delivery, the girl wears a simple blue garment; her head and that of her child are softly haloed. He had earlier rendered Christ crucified in his famous *Yellow Christ*,[26] in which a small pathetic figure seen from a considerable distance hangs from the cross, while local women stand about, expressing through their attitudes of quiet awe their religious response to Christ's suffering. The third painting comprising the triptych depicts Christ's spiritual ordeal at Golgotha in a self-portrait.[27]

In *Light in August* Faulkner also represented—in the view of some critics—a triptych of the Passion.[28] Each of the stories that comprise *Light in August* can, from this point of view, be seen to represent an aspect of the Christ story. Joe Christmas, who is presented in the novel as a figure seen in distanced perspective—his entire life is brought into view in the course of the novel—represents the aspect of Christ which relates to his suffering at the hands of others, i.e., his crucifixion. The simple country girl Lena, in her blue dress, who during the novel gives birth to the son who will be a replacement for Joe Christmas, represents the Nativity. The story of Hightower, the minister, who undergoes an ordeal which is spiritual (and of such an intense nature that it causes the sweat to spring from his

25. Bavarian State Painting Collection, Munich. Reproduced in Robert Goldwater, *Paul Gauguin* (New York: Harry N. Abrams, Inc., n.d.), 136.

26. Albright Art Gallery, Buffalo. In Goldwater, *Paul Gauguin*, 92.

27. Also called *Agony in the Garden*. Norton Gallery and School of Art, West Palm Beach.

28. R. G. Collins, "*Light in August*: Faulkner's Stained Glass Triptych," *Mosaic*, VII (Fall, 1973), 97–157; Ilse Dusoir Lind, "The Calvinistic Burden of *Light in August*," *New England Quarterly*, XXX (September, 1957), 307–29.

brow like blood, as did Christ's at Gethsemane), represents the ordeal in the garden, in which Christ suffered extreme inner torment. The word "autogethsemane," which Gauguin uses as another title for the *Self-Portrait as Christ in Gethsemane*, is used by Faulkner to describe the ordeal of the artist Gordon in *Mosquitoes* (48). In Gauguin's *Self-Portrait with Yellow Christ*,[29] in which he shows the head of the artist in the foreground while a small crucified figure hangs in the background, a relationship exists between the two which parallels the curiously juxtapositional relationship of Hightower and Joe Christmas in Faulkner's novel.

Faulkner went to Europe in 1925 armed with books about art in order to be better able to see what he was looking at. Upon his arrival in Paris, he established himself in a section of the city near the galleries, so that he could conveniently visit them often. In a letter home to his mother he said: "It was very fine, especially the paintings of the more or less moderns—like Degas, Manet and Chavannes."[30]

In the paintings of Degas and Manet, as indicated by observations set down in *Elmer*, Faulkner was aware of the new struggle to render flesh tones accurately, and he was especially sensitive to the new handling of color.[31] Degas's *The Woman Drying Herself*[32] exemplifies these advances, the treatment of color here being related to other innovations. In this painting,

29. Former collection Maurice-Denis. Private collection. Reproduced as frontispiece to Goldwater, *Paul Gauguin*.

30. Blotner, *Faulkner*, I, 454.

31. *Ibid.*, I, 460. "here was Paris . . . where Degas and Monet fought [*sic*?] obscure points of color and life and love, cursing Bougereau and his curved pink flesh" (from the mss. of *Elmer*, as quoted by McHaney, "Elmer Papers": "There was a picture in the Hutchinson galleries that had red in it, that for Elmer was all red. It was by a Frenchman and it may have been a vase of flowers or a woman's dress: he had forgotten which; but from it he had learned that no color has any value, any significance save in relation to other colors seen or suggested or imagined" (47).)

32. Art Institute of Chicago. Reproduced in Daniel Cotton Rich, *Degas* (New York: Harry S. Abrams, n.d.), 124.

in which a red-haired woman's coloring is rendered with great effectiveness, the action of the woman is strongly simplified. Space in the canvas is flattened into a pattern of vivid hues, with various colors crossed by other colors laid over them. In places the paint is several coats thick, Degas allowing glints of color to shine through. The red hair of the woman is shown against an orange patch in the background, in a color study that was stunningly original at the time.

Manet's *In Front of the Mirror* [33] depicts a woman at her mirror, the interest of the painting being centered on the rendering of the flesh tones of her back. Delicacy of coloring is particularly evident in the rendering of the skin. In a closeup view of the canvas, the use of many pastel colors is evident.

The work of Chavannes, often called symbolist because of its strong visionary element, had more than one aspect which Faulkner may have admired. *The Sacred Grove* [34] is an idyllic pastoral which has the quality of a Grecian frieze. *The Poor Fisherman* [35] represents an actual human figure, a man in a small fishing boat just offshore. The quality most admired in *The Poor Fisherman* was the contemplative stillness, the isolation of the various figures in the painting. What is symbolist in quality about this painting is its sense of immanence, its way of suggesting the presence of something haunting and mysterious beyond the power of language to express.

Faulkner also wrote his mother that he had seen the work of Picasso and Matisse in private collections, but without expressing notable enthusiasm. [36] Exploring possible reasons for

33. The Solomon R. Guggenheim Museum, New York. Reproduced in Pierre Schneider, *The World of Manet* (New York: Time-Life Books, n.d.), 9.

34. Reduction of Lyons Mural, 1884. Chicago Art Institute. Slide courtesy Department of Fine Arts, Washington Square and University College of Arts and Sciences, New York University.

35. Éditions des Musées Nationaux, Paris, 1976. Plate No. 58.

36. Blotner, *Faulkner*, I, 454. In James B. Meriwether (ed.), *Essays, Speeches and Public Letters* (New York: Random House, 1965), Faulkner categorizes himself as belonging with artistic experimenters like Matisse and Picas-

this lack of fervor, we learn that Picasso at this time was much more interested in formal relationships within a painting than in the objects depicted. He was currently exhibiting the works of his cubist phase. His *Italian Woman*[37] shows a seated female figure composed of segments that overlap, the emphasis being on the definition of spatial relations. Faulkner gives no evidence at this time of liking this kind of abstraction.

Matisse similarly at this stage had become more interested in the formal relationships within a painting than in the substantive content. In *Goldfish*,[38] for example, the fish in the bowl are of purely decorative interest. The bowl stands on a table before a window, with a dark shutter dividing the window. The treatment is almost cubistic.

Faulkner also mentioned in writing home that he had gone to a very modern exhibition—of futurist and Vorticist paintings —adding that he had been in the company of a painter, "a real one," who said "it's all right to paint the damn things but as for looking at them, he'd rather go to the Luxembourg gardens and watch the children sail their boats."[39] His references to Vorticism, whenever they occur, tend to be slighting, suggesting that he did not accept all the concepts of the Vorticists. His use of the word "cubistic" in *As I Lay Dying* ("The barn door, like a cubistic bug, comes into relief," 209), while it indicates a specific awareness of cubism, is slightly pejorative in tenor, and he gives little evidence of responding to cubism in a strongly positive way. Thus, I do not myself view *As I Lay*

---

so, whose signed works brought unusually high prices. Even here, however, he refers to these two as "special fanciers," *i.e.*, pursuers of a peaceful artistic hobby comparable to the breeding of Dalmatians but carried to an especially rarefied degree (144).

37. E. Buehrle, Zurich. Wilhelm Boeck and Jaime Sabartés (eds.), *Picasso* (New York: Harry N. Abrams, Inc., n.d.), 171.

38. Florence M. Schoenborn–Samuel A. Max Collection, New York City. Reproduced in John Jacobus, *Henri Matisse* (New York: Harry N. Abrams, Inc., n.d.), Colorplate No. 30, p. 144.

39. Blotner, *Faulkner*, I, 453.

*Dying* as being primarily a cubistic work, but rather as a symbolist or even possibly an expressionistic undertaking—as the projection of the thoughts and feelings of many individuals (and of the artist himself) around the idea of dying. The symbolists were very interested in contemplation of the idea of death.

The modern painter Faulkner could not mention without using exclamation marks was Cézanne. His admiration of Cézanne, expressed before he went to Europe, was based on Cézanne's method of painting directly with colored pigments, without the use of guiding structural lines. This is what Faulkner meant when he said that Cézanne dipped his brush in light the way Tobe dips his brush in a paintpot.[40] In Cézanne's *Portrait of Chocquet*[41] this method of painting is visible in the colored brushstrokes. Chocquet was a friend of the impressionists who bought Renoirs and Cézannes before they were generally appreciated. In this portrait, besides capturing his appearance, Cézanne interprets the personality of the man by rendering him as a lean Don Quixote type, an attenuated El Greco figure, symbolizing a person dedicated to an ideal. The coloring throughout the portrait is fresh, with slight red touches in the nose and cheek. An important feature of the painting is that we can see the brushstrokes; we see and follow the action of the brush everywhere. The stroke is intense and direct, with distinct movement in every part. Within the painting as a whole there is a fundamental but unemphasized rhythm of curved lines. Cézanne believed that the basic form in nature was the cone, the basic line circular. It is my belief, based on Faulkner's responses, that he derived much of his sense of curved form from Cézanne. Critics aware of Faulkner's ten-

40. *Ibid.*, 465–66. The precise wording is: "And Cezanne! That man dipped his brush in light like Tobe Caruthers would dip his in red lead to paint a lamp-post."

41. Meyer Schapiro, *Cézanne* (New York: Harry N. Abrams, 1952), 47.

dency to incorporate a sense of curved form into his fiction have coined expressions like "whorls of form" and "spiral form" to give critical expression to this idea.[42] His responses to paintings suggest that he learned more from Cézanne than from the Vorticists, who also believed that circularity was a basic principle in art and nature.

Important also in Cézanne is largeness of effect, the powerful possession of space. The *Portrait of Chocquet*, which seems massive, is only slightly more than eighteen by fourteen inches in size. Faulkner's fiction of the mature phase similarly is characterized by an unusual largeness of effect.

Faulkner's interest in light, as shown in his admiration of Cézanne, is evident throughout his work, in his many twilights and dawns, in his awareness that light is reflected ("from the earth suspired") as well as emitted from the heavens above. The title *Light in August* has reference to a certain quality of light in Mississippi at this time of the year. Throughout Faulkner's work there are constant references to light: things tend to "glow," "glare," "glint," "glimmer," "shine," "gleam," and in other ways to emit or reflect light.

The novelist and photographer Wright Morris once observed that in looking through an album of modern paintings he had a curious sense of déjà vu—the sense that he had experienced it all before when he looked at the work of certain painters like Munch, Van Gogh, Rouault, and Soutine in paintings we now categorize as expressionist, in which the abnormal is carried to a point of hallucination.[43] Here the artist often seems demented, though he is exercising the utmost artistic ingenuity to express feelings beyond the rational. Morris suspected that he had this sense of déjà vu because in reading

42. Donald Tritschler, "The Unity of Faulkner's Shaping Vision," *Modern Fiction Studies* (Winter, 1959–60), 337–43; Phyllis Hirshleifer, "As Whirlwinds in the South: *Light in August*," *Perspective*, II (Summer, 1949), 225–38.

43. Wright Morris, "Violent Land: Some Observations on the Faulkner Country," *Magazine of Art*, XLV (March, 1952), 99–103.

Faulkner he had already experienced the kinds of emotion that these paintings characteristically evoke. In these paintings, which describe strong feelings (especially in relation to sex and rage) Wright said: "the color shrieks, the light glares or burns, faces are red, green, purple or yellow, shapes have the appearance of having been seized and contorted by powerful hands. The artist seems possessed, we sometimes feel, by a raging, inarticulate demon, and the paint itself is possessed by a fervor to express something. The painter does it with paint, but it can also be done with words."[44]

It is interesting to consider bright color, in this connection, as it figures in the work of Faulkner. Hemingway's fiction reveals the use of very little color despite the violence of blood which appears as a theme in his work.[45] In Faulkner, brilliant and intense color often appears. In *As I Lay Dying*, for example (as shown in *The Concordance to the Novel*), Jewel's face "goes from *green* to *red* and *green* again"; Eula's hat is *red*; there is a *red* barn, a *red* road, a *red* flood, a hill of *red* sand. The drugstore window has vials of *red* and *green*. There is also yellow: a *yellow* road, mules splashed with *yellow* mud, lumber which gleams *yellow*. And there is *blue* as well—the horse's eyes are "a mild *baby blue*." There are blue shadows, as well as a hill that dissolves into a "mass of *dark green*" [italics mine]. These colors appear in the text as an element of composition of which we are unconscious; they are strongly expressionistic.

Certain fundamental analogies between works by expressionist painters and elements in Faulkner's work suggested themselves strongly to Wright Morris. Pursuing several of these we find that Munch's *The Cry*,[46] for example, expresses crippled rage through its lone haunted figure. The landscape

44. *Ibid.*, 99.

45. Emily Stipes Watts, *Ernest Hemingway and the Arts* (Urbana: University of Illinois Press), 36.

46. National Gallery, Oslo. Thomas M. Messer, *Edvard Munch* (New York: Harry N. Abrams, Inc., n.d.), Illustration No. 17, p. 85.

itself here seems to dissolve into a shuddering wail. Bands of color, resembling sound waves, express an unforgettable cry of agony. Analogously, Benjy's voice at the end of *The Sound and the Fury* is the ultimate in vocalized despair. It was "the grave hopeless sound of all misery under the sun" (332). "There was more than astonishment in it, it was horror; agony eyeless; tongueless; just sound" (335).

Van Gogh's *Landscape with Olive Trees*[47] is an example of a violent landscape resembling Faulkner's own violent land. In this canvas the passion of the painter seems to fill the entire landscape—ground, trees, clouds, mountains—with a tumultuous motion. Long wavy lines go across the canvas. The movement seems to come from an underlying force that affects all objects. Evident in the canvas are the strokes of the brush, as in Cézanne, but they are far more furious.

Rouault's *Red-Haired Woman*,[48] which shows a prostitute at her mirror, expresses through its heavy and dark outlines the painter's rage at the social system which creates and exploits the prostitute. Rouault's *The Old King*[49] conveys through its opulent colors the weight of civilization borne by the old king. In his hand, he holds a flower, which he contemplates. In his gaze at the flower and his sadness, he puts us in mind of Benjy holding a narcissus in *The Sound and the Fury.*

Soutine's *The Slain Cock*,[50] painted after the artist had made a suicide attempt, is another example of an expressionistic painting which has a Faulknerian intensity. This painting renders the emotion of total despair. The head hangs down,

47. Collection of John Hay Whitney. Meyer Schapiro, *Vincent Van Gogh* (New York: Harry N. Abrams, Inc., n.d.), 108.

48. Musée National d'Art Moderne, Paris. Reproduced in Pierre Courthion (ed.), *Georges Rouault* (New York: Harry N. Abrams, Inc., n.d.), 83.

49. Carnegie Institute, Pittsburgh. Reproduced in Courthion (ed.), *Georges Rouault*, 239.

50. Chicago Art Institute. Slide copy, courtesy Washington Square and University College of Arts and Sciences, New York University.

the prevailing color is that of spilled blood, and the breast is plucked bare of feathers, though the wings still have them.

Every reader of Faulkner who is interested in modern painting associates certain twentieth-century masterpieces with images in Faulkner's work. To me, Uncle Buck and Uncle Buddy playing poker in "Was" suggest Cézanne's *The Card-players*.[51] This painting, which exemplified the way Cézanne painted the local but transcended it, suggests the same quality in Faulkner's art. Here because of the contemplativeness of the players, their absorbed attitudes, they seem to be universal cardplayers. Similarly, the Cézanne landscape *Mountains in Provence*,[52] which shows a field divided up by cultivation of various sections, the entire landscape being viewed from an aerial perspective, puts me in mind of Sutpen's view of plantation land, "all divided up and fixed and neat" (221) because of the color that people's skins happen to be.

In *Light in August*, Joe Christmas recalls his early life as resembling a "big long garbled cold echoing building of dark red brick" (104), and Christmas himself is described as the ultimate in human loneliness as he walks alone down a deserted Jefferson street. These, and other references to "barren corridors" and empty "gray tunnels," arouse associations with the early paintings of de Chirico. It was de Chirico's triumph that, through his renderings of empty buildings and depopulated places casting stark shadows, he was able to depict human isolation as a spiritual condition. In some instances, he combined barren buildings with clock faces in such a way as to express both an alienated emotional state and obsession with time, making us think of Quentin's mental state in *The Sound and the Fury*.[53]

51. Musée du Louvre, Paris. Reproduced in Schapiro, *Cézanne*, 88.

52. Tate Gallery, London. Reproduced in Schapiro, *Cézanne*, 78.

53. Isabella Farr, *Chirico* (New York: Harry N. Abrams, Inc., 1968), *Enigma of the Hour*, Plate No. 20.

The Effect of Painting on Faulkner's Poetic Form

The nature of the Protestant religious experience is one of the major subjects explored in *Light in August*; as a consequence, the image of the village church as seen by Hightower in the final chapter is particularly significant. Hightower pictures his Presbyterian church and the churches of other Protestant denominations in Jefferson as projecting their spires sharply into the sky, in a progression that is "endless, without order, empty, symbolic, bleak, skypointed not with ecstasy or passion but in abjuration, threat, and doom" (426). This unusual image calls to mind the angularity of Feininger's painting *Village Church* (1928).[54] Feininger painted his own church at Gelmerode on many occasions and in many moods. The highly abstracted treatment of *Village Church* (1928), with its many "skypointed" lines and color treatment based on prism theory, expresses both the criticism of the church and respect for its unrealized potential which is expressed by Faulkner's concluding image.

Faulkner never lost his intense reaction to art. In 1950, when Bob Haas and his wife casually invited Faulkner to join them in a visit to a Rembrandt exhibit at the Wildenstein Gallery in New York, Faulkner—to their surprise—agreed to join them. They were amazed to see how rapt he was before the pictures. Afterwards, when they returned to the Haas's home and took down a Rembrandt book, they were even more amazed to discover that Faulkner seemed to have remembered everything he saw. Faulkner was stirred by his view of the Rembrandts and later that evening he told them the entire story of *A Fable*.[55]

During their visit to the gallery, the Haas's consciousness of being in the presence of a famous author caused them to note

54. Rev. Dr. Laurence Feininger, Trento, Italy. Painting inaccessible. Reproduced in Hans Hess, *Lyonel Feininger* (New York: Harry N. Abrams, Inc., n.d.), 275.
55. Blotner, *Faulkner*, II, 1307.

some of the pictures that particularly engaged his attention. Among these were the famous Rembrandt *Self-Portrait (1659–60),*[56] one of the many notable studies in which Rembrandt analyzed his own moral and physical progress. Also of interest to Faulkner were the many pictures with biblical subjects. Rembrandt's outstanding quality as an interpreter of the Bible was his tendency not to separate the human point of view from the pictorial. He rendered his characters in a way that showed his intimate and loving knowledge of the Bible stories and his inclination to associate biblical characters with people belonging to the run of ordinary humanity. Rembrandt's treatment of biblical subjects parallels Faulkner's own when he utilizes biblical myth in his work.

Faulkner's visit to the Wildenstein Gallery made him think of *A Fable,* and *A Fable,* specifically, is brought to mind by the Bible pictures Faulkner saw at the exhibit. For example, Rembrandt in his Christ pictures conveys a strong sense of the military context; there are always Roman soldiers present, waiting to take Christ in or to bring pressure on others to betray him. In *A Fable,* the military hierarchy represents all institutions that wield power over individual men; an ongoing conflict exists between the military establishment and Christ. Various other etchings and drawings by Rembrandt are also suggestive in relation to *A Fable. Christ Mocked,*[57] a small etching in the exhibit, stressed Christ's isolation through emphasis upon the way the figures are crowded on the left of Christ, while a considerable interval of space is left between Jesus and the man on the right. The theme of Christ mocked appears in *A Fable* at the opening of the novel, when the corporal must bear alone the vituperation which the kin of the mutinous regiment heap

56. Reproduced in Bob Haak, *Rembrandt, His Life, His Work, His Time* (New York: Harry N. Abrams, Inc., n.d.), Illustration No. 479, p. 288.

57. Formerly Léon Bonnat Collection, Paris; present whereabouts of this drawing unknown. Reproduced in Seymour Slive, *Drawings of Rembrandt* (New York: Dover Publications, 1965), II, Illustration No. 353.

upon him. *St. Peter Denying Christ*,[58] a drawing for a study of the painting, shows St. Peter replying to the interrogations of the Roman soldiers. In *A Fable*, Faulkner also includes a symbolic Peter (as well as a Judas) among his disciples. Rembrandt's drawing *The Arrest of Christ*[59] shows Christ's divinity rendered by the technique of physical enlargement of his stature to a point where it is about twice the size of the soldiers who have come to arrest him. Holy light radiates from him. In *A Fable*, the corporal is presented as a Messiah whose powerful personal presence alone is sufficient to arouse the spirituality of the soldiers around him and to inspire them to unite in their desire for peace.

The Christ theme which pervades Faulkner's work derives primarily from his religious background; at the same time, it is influenced by religious art (as illustrated in Eli Faure's *Outlines of the History of Art* and as seen elsewhere). It therefore lends itself to iconographical study. Faulkner's manner of treating Christian themes, in other words, can profitably be compared to the treatment of such themes in the visual arts. While the purpose of describing Faulkner's visit to the Wildenstein Gallery here has been primarily to demonstrate that his interest in art was still vital even during the later stages of his literary career, it also serves as a reminder that his creativity in this realm, though seemingly dormant, still exerted a significant creative influence on his fiction.

58. École des Beaux-Arts, Paris. In Slive, *Drawings of Rembrandt*, I, Illustration No. 146.

59. Count Antoine Seilern Collection, London. In Slive, *Drawings of Rembrandt*, I, Illustration No. 271.

# *Tomorrow*: The Genesis
of a Screenplay

## HORTON FOOTE

When Herbert Brodkin sent me the short story "Tomorrow," I hadn't remembered reading it before although I had read most of the other stories in the collection *Knight's Gambit*. I found myself interested but having almost the opposite reaction than I had when I first read "Old Man." My chief concern was would there be enough material for a ninety-minute television play. As is the way with television and particularly television at that time, they were most anxious to have a quick decision from me, and my first inclination was to say that I really didn't feel that I could undertake it, that there was nothing there really that I felt I might do justice to. However, I found myself all afternoon postponing this decision and thinking more and more about certain elements of the story. I do remember being very intrigued by the character of Fentry, and the way that Faulkner undertook to tell his story. It is told from three points of view—four really, if you count Gavin Stevens, who is mostly a listener, but at times expresses a point of view and some facts. Each of the narrators is important to the story because each one has knowledge of certain events that the others can't possibly know, and there is an erratic time sequence.

I'd like to quote now from an interview I gave after I dramatized a Flannery O'Connor story. The interviewer asked if there was anything about the day-by-day working when you're attempting an adaptation that is different from when you're working on an original script. I answered,

Yes, when you are working on something of your own, it's like going into an uncharted world, and part of the secret is to find the form, the structure. When you are restructuring a story in dramatic form, you are involved in the process of construction, but there are so many things that you assimilate differently. When you're working on something of your own, you call upon a lot of unconscious things that you have been storing up and thinking about. Well, here a great deal more is conscious, and you have to approach consciously what must have been an unconscious process for the original writer. But there are times . . . for instance, when I was dramatizing Faulkner's story, "Tomorrow," the character of the woman became alive to me, even though Faulkner gives only a few paragraphs to her. He told me enough about her so that my imagination just began to work, and she became somebody I knew.

These are the paragraphs I was referring to that first made me really want to enter the world of Jackson Fentry:

Then one afternoon in February—there had been a mild spell and I reckon I was restless—I rode out there. [It's the Quick boy talking.] The first thing I seen was her, and it was the first time I had ever done that—a woman, young, and maybe when she was in her normal health she might have been pretty, too; I don't know. Because she wasn't just thin, she was gaunted. She was sick, more than just starved-looking, even if she was still on her feet, and it wasn't just because she was going to have that baby in a considerable less than another month. And I says, "Who is that?" and he looked at me and says, "That's my wife," and I says, "Since when? You never had no wife last fall. And that child ain't a month off." And he says, "Do you want us to leave?" and I says, "What do I want you to leave for?" I'm going to tell this from what I know now, what I found out after them two brothers showed up here three years later with their court paper, not from what ever he told me, because he never told nobody nothing. . . . I don't know where he found her. I don't know if he found her somewhere, or if she just walked into the mill one day or one night and he looked up and seen her, and it was like the fellow says—nobody knows where or when love or lightning either is going to strike, except that it ain't going to strike there twice, because it don't have to. . . . and I don't believe she was scared or ashamed to go back home just because her brothers and father had tried to keep her from marrying the husband, in the first place. I believe it was just some more of that same kind of black-complected and not extra-intelligent and pretty durn ruthless blood pride that them brothers themselves was waving around here about an hour that day.

Anyway, there she was, and I reckon she knowed her time was going to be short, and him saying to her, "Let's get married," and her saying, "I can't marry you. I already got a husband." And her time come and she was down then, on that shuck mattress, and him feeding her with the spoon, likely, and I reckon she knowed she wouldn't get up from it, and he got the midwife, and the baby was born, and likely her and the midwife both knowed by then she would never get up from that mattress and maybe they even convinced him at last, or maybe she knowed it wouldn't make no difference nohow and said yes, and he taken the mule pap let him keep at the mill and rid seven miles to Preacher Whitfield's and brung Whitfield back about daylight, and Whitfield married them and she died, and him and Whitfield buried her. And that night he come to the house and told pap he was quitting, and left the mule, and I went out to the mill a few days later and he was gone—

And I dramatized their meeting this way:

> ISHAM *goes out the door.* FENTRY *has finished the little food he prepared for himself. He scrapes the dish outside the door and then starts outside to wash the dishes, when he hears a noise. It is the low moan of someone in pain. He stands listening for a moment; the sound comes again. He steps outside the door and calls.*)

FENTRY: Isham. Isham.
> (*There is no answer to his call. The sound comes again and he walks toward it. He goes over to a stack of lumber inside an open shed. Lying against the logs is a young woman,*

151

*black-haired, poorly dressed, thin, gaunt, almost emaciated, her clothes patched and worn and no protection at all against the cold. If she were not so ill and starved-looking, she might be pretty. Even so, there is pride and dignity in her face. He goes over to her and gently rolls her over on her back. It is then that we see she is pregnant. He sees how cold her thin arms and legs are and takes his coat off and puts it over her. It is difficult to tell at first whether she is alive or dead, and he stands for a moment looking at the careworn, hurt face. He feels her pulse and knows then that she is living. He watches her for a moment longer and then, shaking her gently, he tries to rouse her.)*

FENTRY: Lady. Lady.

*(He gets no response. He goes to the well, gets a dipper of water, comes back with the water, and pats her face gently with it. She opens her eyes slowly.)*

SARAH: Where am I?

FENTRY: You're at Ben Quick's saw mill over at Frenchman's Bend. *(He looks down at the thin, emaciated face.)* I'm Jackson Fentry. I'm the watchman out here in the winter time when the mill is shut down. I heard you when I came out the door of the boiler room. You sounded to me like you was in pain. Are you in pain? *(The woman shakes her head weakly, "No." She shivers and he puts his coat more securely around her.)* How long have you been here?

SARAH: I don't know. I remember walking down the road back yonder. I don't remember passing the saw mill. I knowed I was feeling dizzy, and I said to myself, I hope I ain't going to faint, but I guess I did. Though when I did, and how I got here, I don't exactly remember. *(She rests her head back on the logs.)* What day is it?

FENTRY: Christmas Eve.

SARAH: Is it the morning or the afternoon?

FENTRY: It's the late morning.

SARAH: Then I haven't been here too long. It was early in the morning on Christmas Eve when I started this way. *(She tries to get up.)*

FENTRY: Let me help you.

SARAH: Thank you. I think I'd better be getting on now. *(He helps her up, but she is still very weak and has to lean against the pile of logs and against Fentry.)* I'm sorry. I guess I will have to rest a while longer. I haven't quite gotten my strength back.

FENTRY: Let me help you in here so you can rest by my fire. It's so raw and cold out here.
SARAH: Thank you. It has been a cold winter, hasn't it?
FENTRY: Yes'm.
SARAH: There was ice this morning early when I left the house. I seen it on the ditches as I passed.
FENTRY: Yes'm.
SARAH: I said to myself, Jack Frost has been here.
FENTRY: He sure had. (*She is gasping for breath and holds on to him. They pause for a moment.*)
SARAH: How far we got to go?
FENTRY: Just in this door here. Can you make it?
SARAH: Yes sir. I can make that. (*They start on again slowly. They reach the doorway. She rests again by the doorway for a moment.*) Thank you. You say it's warm in here?
FENTRY: Oh, yes, ma'am. (*He helps her inside the door and to the chair. She sits slowly down and rests her head against the back as if this little exertion was made at great cost.* You set here, Mrs. ——.
SARAH: Thank you. (*She looks around.*) It is nice and warm in here. I love a good fire in the stove.
FENTRY: I could get it warmer. I was letting it die out because I was about to leave for my Papa's farm for Christmas. (*He goes to the stove and starts to feed it wood.*)

Now, I know a lot about cotton fields; I know nothing about sawmills. In any case, I began somehow in the most obsessive, vivid kind of way to want to discover for myself, as a writer, what went on between Jackson Fentry and this black-complected woman.

It's interesting that both actresses, Kim Stanley and Olga Bellin, who have played Sarah are blonde, but they did understand the fierce pride of the woman, "black-complected pride" Faulkner calls it. I called this woman Sarah, although Faulkner never names her and I had her married to a man named Eubanks. And so that night I sat down and I began to dramatize what I felt was the story of Jackson Fentry and Sarah Eubanks. I worked on it that night and finished it early the next

153

morning. And from that time until this, I have never changed it. It seemed to me moving, but I realized that what I had written was monstrously out of proportion to the rest of the story. I wanted to retain this, and I wanted to see it used so I began to construct the rest of the play around the story of these two people. In looking back over the original copy of the story that I worked with, I find that I have marked these paragraphs.

The first one reads:

And the story itself was old and unoriginal enough: The country girl of seventeen, her imagination fired by the swagger and the prowess and the daring and the glib tongue; the father who tried to reason with her and got as far as parents usually do in such cases; then the interdiction, the forbidden door, the inevitable elopement at midnight; and at four o'clock the next morning Bookwright waked Will Varner, the justice of the peace and the chief officer of the district, and handed Varner his pistol and said, "I have come to surrender. I killed Thorpe two hours ago." And a neighbor named Quick, who was first on the scene, found the half-drawn pistol in Thorpe's hand; and a week after the brief account was printed in the Memphis papers, a woman appeared in Frenchman's Bend who claimed to be Thorpe's wife, and with the wedding license to prove it, trying to claim what money or property he might have left.

Now surely if one had the imagination, a whole play could be done on the basis of that one paragraph. It is curious that I have marked it because in every attempt that I have made to dramatize "Tomorrow," I have always in some measure tried to use effectively that element of the story which has to do with Buck Thorpe as a grown man and, in all candor, I don't think I've ever found a way to integrate it into any version I have done, as well as Faulkner has done in his short story.

The next paragraphs marked are these:

"I went close enough," Pruitt said. "I would get close enough to the field to hear him cussing at the nigger for not moving fast enough and to watch the nigger trying to keep up with him, and to think what a good thing it was Jackson hadn't got two niggers to work the place while he was gone, because if that old man—and he was close to sixty by then—had had to spend one full day sitting in a chair in the shade with nothing in his hands to chop or hoe with, he would have died before sundown. So Jackson left. He walked. They didn't have but one mule. They ain't never had but one mule. But it ain't but about thirty miles. He was gone about two and a half years. Then one day ———"

"He came that first Christmas," Mrs. Pruitt said.

"That's right," Pruitt said. "He walked them thirty miles home and spent Christmas Day and walked them other thirty miles back to the sawmill."

"Whose sawmill," Uncle Gavin said.

"Quick's," Pruitt said. "Old Man Ben Quick's. It was the second Christmas he never come home. Then, about the beginning of March, about when the river bottom at Frenchman's Bend would be starting to dry out where you could skid logs through it and you would have thought he would be settled down good to his third year of saw-milling, he come home to stay. He didn't walk this time. He come in a hired buggy. Because he had the goat and the baby."

And then later Pruitt says:

"In the next summer, him and the boy disappeared."

"Disappeared?" Uncle Gavin said.

"That's right. They were just gone one morning. I didn't know when. And one day I couldn't stand it no longer, I went up there and the house was empty, and I went on to the field where the old man was plowing, and at first I thought the spreader between his plow handles had broke and he had tied a sapling across the handles, until he seen me and snatched the sapling off, and it was that shotgun, and I reckon what he said to me was about what he said to you this morning when you stopped there. Next year he had the nigger helping him again. Then, about five years later, Jackson come back I don't know when. He was just there one morning. And the nigger was gone again, and him and his pa worked the place like they used to. And one day I couldn't stand it no longer, I went up there and I stood at the fence where he was plowing, until after a while the land he was breaking brought him up to the fence, and still he had never looked at me; he plowed right by me, not ten feet away, still without looking at me, and he turned and come back, and I said, 'Did he die, Jackson?' and then he looked at me. 'The boy,' I said. And he said, 'What boy?' "

They invited us to stay for dinner.

Uncle Gavin thanked them. "We brought a snack with us," he said. "And it's thirty miles to Varner's store, and twenty-two from there to Jefferson. And our roads ain't used to automobiles yet."

I am not really sure now why I marked those paragraphs when first attempting to dramatize "Tomorrow," but I am very moved now when I read this description of the father. I think that I wanted to try and retain in the character this wonderful sense that Faulkner can give us of a man and his need to work, his total absorption into whatever has been given him to do and his ability to live in solitude under the most primitive and unlikely conditions. That that man can also express pride, loyalty, integrity, and many most admirable virtues and that Faulkner always finds a way to give us these qualities in a very unsentimental way. I think I was successful in doing this in the television and stage versions. In the latter paragraph, I suspect I was interested in the relationship of the neighbors to the story—how they had to know what was going on and what means they had to use to find out what was going on. I've always been haunted by the question that Pruitt asked Fentry after he had returned and the boy had been taken from him: "That boy?" he asks. And Fentry's answer: "What boy?"

One of the obvious problems in dramatizing this story is the matter of time. In "The Old Man," although the story was also told out of sequence, time was very defined from the beginning of the flood to the end of the flood. Here time, although it is approached in various ways, and not in sequence, roughly goes over a period of twenty years or more. This makes enormous technical difficulties, first of all, on the actor to convinc-

ingly play a time span of twenty years even though Jackson
Fentry would always seem to have very specific characteristics
that were almost timeless; in other words, one would imagine
that as a young man, he already seemed old, and that as an
older man he did not change much. Still, there was a question
of the characters around him aging naturally as one does in the
span of twenty years. At first this was a great worry to me but
then I decided that, again, this was not really my problem and
that what I had to address myself to was dramatizing, as best I
could, the story Faulkner had given me and to let the director
and the producer take care of the solving of those problems in
their casting of my play. I decided therefore to begin with the
search of the lawyer, Gavin Stevens. Why had a Mississippi
dirt farmer named Jackson Fentry hung his jury? Instead of
three characters telling the story of Fentry to Stevens, I decided to confine it to the Pruitts. It was apparent that, given the
character of Fentry, Stevens would never go directly to him,
and I felt that in terms of my structure, that it would be best
served by one point of view or narrator, if you will. And so,
these choices—the choice of where to begin the story, the choice
of dramatizing very fully the relationship of Sarah Eubanks
and Jackson Fentry, the choice of the Pruitts as narrator, the
choice of trying to accommodate in some way Faulkner's time
structure—all dictated the form that finally began to evolve as
the first version of "Tomorrow."

There was always in this version, for me, a worrisome problem. The more completely I dramatized the relationship between Fentry and Sarah, the less room it left for the dramatizing of the other elements of the story. I finished the first version
of the story—my dramatization of it—very quickly in four or
five days. Brodkin read it and immediately called to say that
he liked it and wanted to do it. It was scheduled for six weeks
from the time of acceptance; there was casting to be done but
I had that time then to think about any further changes or im-

provements I wanted to make. Most of my thinking, as I remember, was spent in wondering what happened to Fentry from the time he left the cotton farm after the boy he adopted had been taken away from him until the time when he returned, and I made a very logical sequence of events for myself but none of it was I able to use dramatically in the structure of the play.

The other element that I felt I was never able fully to solve satisfactorily for myself, in any version, was how to dramatically use the return of the grown Buck Thorpe, and how to dramatize properly the telling of Fentry about him and what happened when Fentry decides to see for himself the spectacle of the evolution of Buck Thorpe.

In all versions, in television and the theater and on the screen, we attempted this meeting. I think it was most effective in the theater. There was something immediate and quite wonderful about the meeting of the two in the scene that we found in the play version. In the screen version, the scene was shot and I understand that it was very difficult for Bob Duvall, that it was not in the final cut of the screenplay, because he felt so strongly that in some ways, it was his best work, and the producer and the director told me that they did indeed agree that it was.

After I finished my work on the television play, I had a meeting with Robert Mulligan, who was to direct it. He liked what I had done but he felt that it would lack—which is a term that I've heard often in my life—theatrical excitement. His first suggestion to give it theatrical excitement was to somehow start with the trial and try to build the story from there. I had earlier thought of starting the play with the trial, but given the ninety minutes (or seventy minutes really allotted for playing time) it had seemed to me uneconomical. Anyway, I tried again for four or five days, but felt it was no improvement over

158

my beginning, so it was agreed to return to what I had already written.

I started the play on the front porch of the Pruitts' farmhouse. Ed Pruitt and his mother are there and they see Thornton Douglas's car come up the road. (I had to change Gavin Stevens to Thornton Douglas for legal reasons.)

MRS. PRUITT: Whose car is that coming up the road?
PRUITT: I think it's Lawyer Douglas's son's car.
MRS. PRUITT: What's he doing around here this time of morning?
(*The car stops.*)
PRUITT: Looks to me like he's coming to see us.
MRS. PRUITT: What's he want with us?
PRUITT: He probably is going to ask us some questions about Jackson Fentry.
MRS. PRUITT: Don't you tell him nothing, Pruitt.
PRUITT: Yes'm.
(*Thornton Douglas, thirty, and his nephew, Charles, fourteen, come up to the porch.*)
THORNTON: Howdy.
PRUITT: Howdy, Thornton.
THORNTON: How are you, Mrs. Pruitt?
MRS. PRUITT: Pretty well.
THORNTON: You're looking very well.
MRS. PRUITT: Thank you, I can't complain.
THORNTON: This is my nephew, Charles. He's my partner, aren't you, boy?
CHARLES: Yes, sir.
THORNTON: He likes to ride out in the country with me.
MRS. PRUITT: Hello, son.
THORNTON: I don't know if you folks know it or not, but I'm a lawyer now.
PRUITT: Yes sir. We heard.

And then Douglas begins to tell them why he's here. He uses in this speech a great deal of the material Faulkner gives him when making his jury summation. And the Pruitts change their mind and decide to tell him what he wants to know about Jackson Fentry, and they begin their story on the night Fentry tells them he is going away to work in a sawmill and to ask them to look in on his father while he's gone. And I followed the action directly until the end of the story, using Pruitt as a "voice over" to make certain scene transitions or give us facts we needed to know.

We had a fine cast: Richard Boone was Fentry; Kim Stanley, perhaps our finest actress, was Sarah; Beulah Bondi, the midwife; Chill Wills, Pruitt; Elizabeth Patterson, Mrs. Pruitt; Charles Bickford, Papa Fentry.

It was first produced on "Playhouse 90," March 7, 1960, and repeated again July 18, 1961. It was done in the studio live and in sequence.

Some years later Herbert Berghof called me about doing the play in his small Off-Broadway theater on Bank Street in New York. He said his production would be based on the idea of compressed time. I didn't quite understand what he meant then (I talked to him about it again a few days ago and I'm not sure I still understand), but I have great respect for his directorial talents and I agreed to let him do it. He wanted to use my play basically as it was done on television with the exception of using Thornton Douglas rather than Pruitt as our narrator, and starting the play with Douglas's speech to the jury, or part of it, and having him address the audience as if they were the jury. He was casting Robert Duvall in the role of Fentry and Olga Bellin as Sarah.

I was living in New Hampshire then and only came to a run-through in the last week. I was very impressed with the work of the director and the actors. It was his production that Paul Roebling and Gilbert Pearlman saw. A few weeks later, they called to ask me about doing it as a film and if I would care to do the screenplay. They wanted to use Robert Duvall and Olga Bellin in the two parts.

In our first discussions, they both said that the presence of Sarah Eubanks, which was so felt in the first part of the story as I dramatized it, should somehow be kept in the second part. So I took that as a kind of task for myself. Then, of course, there's always the notion of having enormous visual and physical freedom with the camera, which was not allowed to me in theater or television. They wanted to do it on location in Mississippi, and they wanted to make it as authentic as possible, and they said they would do everything they could to maintain that authenticity.

The screenplay we went into rehearsal with had a great deal of material in the second half of the film trying to keep the memory of Sarah alive, but most of it was cut in the rehearsals before the filming began. There were additions: we started the film in the courthouse and the trial; we used the jury, we had Douglas address the jury, witnessed Fentry hang the jury, and from there went out into the country with Douglas as he began his search for why Fentry had done this. We took Fentry and Sarah outside the cabin as much as possible, dramatizing the moment when he shows where he hopes to build her house. We added the scene between Sarah and Fentry when it is raining and she speculates about walking on water; after Sarah dies, Fentry's trip home with the baby and the goat; and many new scenes between Fentry and the boy.

A film has its own rhythm, its own life. Joseph Anthony, the director, has a wonderful sense of detail, the kind of detail that makes the life on screen believable; the details were valuable and interesting but they took a great deal of time. The first cut of the film was extremely long; Roebling, Pearlman, and Anthony worked many hours with Reva Schlesinger, the cutter. All the Pruitt scenes were cut, most of Papa Fentry's scenes were cut. What was retained (there had been some cuts here in rehearsals) were the scenes between Fentry and Sarah. There were substitutions: the boy playing Jackson and Longstreet was not a trained actor and was very shy. Duvall spent many hours with him on the set and off winning his confidence. When it came to the actual shooting of the scenes, however, he would become stiff and self-conscious when he had to say the dialogue. So Duvall—and he is a master at this—simply improvised the scenes with him using whatever the boy said spontaneously.

The film was shot on location here in Mississippi with extremely limited funds. *The Reivers* had just been here with a great deal of money to spend, and when we came along with no money, we weren't, at first, believed. The town of Tupelo was finally cooperative and helpful in every way. We found our sawmill out in the country and used a building provided by the town for our shooting in case of rain. The courthouse, at Jacinto, then being restored, was in an adjoining county; our costumes were loaned to us by the University of Mississippi; and we used many local people as actors and extras.

The film has been shown in many festivals; it is in the film collection in the Museum of Modern Art and in Paris. It has had much critical success, but distributors are wary of it and it has been seen by relatively few people. It was revived recently by Joseph Papp for twenty-four performances in his film series at the Public Theatre in New York, and I understand all performances were sold out so maybe it will finally be given a chance to reach a larger audience.

# Faulkner's Film Career:
# The Years with Hawks

BRUCE KAWIN

Once upon a time the greatest American novelist of the twentieth century sat in the office of a producer or director at Warner Brothers—no one seems to remember which—outlining a
story. There was a man and a horse in it; the horse did so-and-
so, and the man and the horse so-and-so, and then the horse . . .
"Bill, forget it," interrupted the bigshot. "We don't want the
horse, at all. Just forget the horse. Come up with something
else." Faulkner puffed on his pipe for a long time, then finally
said, "How about a mule?"

He grinned when he said it—not just at the wit of his own
remark, I imagine, but also because of the pleasure of asserting
that he was now and had ever been William Faulkner, southern writer, a man more familiar with mules than with Hollywood traffic jams, metaphysician of the Mississippi microcosm.

There is no question that Faulkner would not have worked
in Hollywood if he had not needed the money, nor that he
often felt alienated and unhappy there. There is some question
whether he took film seriously as an art. When I asked Meta
Wilde about that, she told me the mule story and then observed that if Faulkner had considered film a worthwhile art
form, he would *never* have agreed to work on *Land of the
Pharaohs*; he had done so, she said, simply because his friend
Howard Hawks needed help and would pay him. On the other
hand, Faulkner knew enough about the art to single out Jean

Renoir as the best director of his generation, and respected Hawks as a strong and efficient storyteller—not as some hack.

The work Faulkner did in Hollywood breaks generally into two categories: the good work he did for good directors who took him seriously, and the hack work he did for the rest. Some of that hack work is enjoyable—the love and dueling scenes in the Errol Flynn *Adventures of Don Juan*, for instance, and even some parts of *Land of the Pharaohs*—but most of it did not reach the screen. There is a middle ground, too, comprised of minor contributions to such reasonably good films as *Mildred Pierce*, *Air Force*, *Drums Along the Mohawk*, and *Gunga Din*. But the good work—and my point here is that there is a great deal of good work—divides further into two categories: what got filmed, and what did not. Among the unproduced screenplays authored entirely by Faulkner are *War Birds* (the missing link between *Flags in the Dust* and *The Unvanquished*), *Dreadful Hollow* (a brilliant horror story of the Val Lewton variety, but written for Hawks), *Country Lawyer* (a multigenerational down-home *Romeo and Juliet*), and *Stallion Road* (the film was made from someone else's script). There is no produced film that is "100 percent scripted by Faulkner," since those scripts were usually written in collaboration and modified during shooting, but his contributions to *The Southerner*, *Today We Live*, *The Road to Glory*, *To Have and Have Not*, and *The Big Sleep* are very significant, and the films are well-made and interesting.

I consider it a matter of some importance that Faulkner's best Hollywood work be published, so that the full range of his career can be appreciated and enjoyed. *War Birds* and *Dreadful Hollow* are solid and powerful works, and I can imagine no letters or juvenilia or alternate drafts of novels that would be as useful and interesting to students of Faulkner as is his second draft of *Today We Live* (*Turn About*). (I say this after having spent more than a year trying, so far unsuccessfully, to

164

interest Random House in the project, and any lobbying by this audience would be appreciated.) Although his screenplays are not formally experimental, many of them are in the first place solidly professional and in the second place closely related to the themes of his major fiction. One does not have to be told, looking over these scripts, that Faulkner took a good deal of his Hollywood work seriously, and used it as a vehicle for some of his major thematic concerns. It is well known that he got the idea for *A Fable* from a script conference with Henry Hathaway and William Bacher (though that is an oversimplification; Hawks's 1943 *Battle Cry*, which had just been abandoned during preproduction, was also a relevant influence), but it is less well known that the ethical renewal outlined in "An Odor of Verbena" originated in *War Birds* (1933), and the relations between *Sutter's Gold* and *Absalom, Absalom!* have never even been discussed. What I should like to do here is to give a brief overview of Faulkner's film career and to introduce *Today We Live* and *The Road to Glory*.

The story of Faulkner the screenwriter is fundamentally that of his relationship with Howard Hawks. That story begins, ironically enough, with Hawks's reading *Soldiers' Pay* around 1929 and telling some of his New York writer friends that they ought to become familiar with the work of the then unknown Faulkner, whom Hawks identified at the time as one of the country's best authors. It is entirely reasonable to suggest that Hawks had a lot to do with Faulkner's becoming known in the literary community in the first place. The publication of *Sanctuary* in 1931 made its author both famous and notorious, and led to his being offered a short-term writing contract at MGM. Hawks had considered filming *Sanctuary* but felt the censorship problem would be too great; Paramount's whitewashed version of that novel, *The Story of Temple Drake* (1933), indirectly vindicates that judgment. At MGM Faulkner wrote several treatments (short narratives with occasional outlined

165

scenes) for films that were not produced, a screenplay about Latin American revolutionaries, and some pages for a film in production (*Lazy River*); none of these warranted his contract's being renewed, although some of the treatments, especially *Absolution*, are interesting and might have made good films. That contract was renewed, however, at the insistence of Hawks, who had finally found a Faulkner story he thought he could adapt: "Turn About," published in the *Saturday Evening Post* and called to his attention by his brother William. At this point I'll let Hawks tell the story of their meeting:

He came in. I said, "My name's Hawks," and he said, "I saw it on a check." He lit a pipe and I said, "Well, I'd like to have you do your story, 'Turn About.'" And he didn't say a damn word and I began to get mad, you know. So I talked for 45 minutes about what I wanted to do, and said, "That's it." He got up. I said, "Where are you going?" "Going in to write. I'm going to write it." So I said, "When will I see you again?" He said, "About five days." I said, "Mr. Faulkner, it shouldn't take you five days to get started and then come back and talk to me," and he said, "No, I can *write* it in five days." And I said, "Well now, look, really, I *found* you because I read a book a long time ago, that you'd written—*Soldiers' Pay.*"[1]

At this point Hawks digressed to tell me how he alerted the literary intelligentsia that flocked around Hecht and MacArthur in New York to Faulkner's existence; I gathered from the way he said it that he had also told this story during that first interview in 1932. Then he went on:

So, Bill said it would take him five days to do the script. And I said, "Okay, would you like a drink?" He said, "Yes." Well, we woke up in a motel in Culver City the next morning. He was fishing cigarette stubs out of a mint julep glass. And in five days he came in with the script. And we became good friends—we liked to fish, we liked to

1. Excerpts from an unpublished interview, Hawks and Kawin, Palm Springs, California, May 24, 1976.

166

hunt. When he needed money, he always used to call me and say, "Do you have anything for me to do?" and if I didn't, I'd make up something.

That first temporary screenplay, written in five days, has not survived. When I was at MGM, I found the second version, *Turn About*, but not the third, *Today We Live*. (I arranged for MGM and 20th Century-Fox to loan xeroxes of all those scripts I could identify as Faulkner's to the University of Virginia's Alderman Library, in case anyone wants to examine these materials. The Warner Brothers materials are still, thanks to the efforts of a few of their lawyers, virtually unavailable.) The story of the revision of *Turn About* reveals much about the process of collaboration, manipulation, and creation in Hollywood, and also shows that Faulkner was willing to do what Hawks wanted.

The original story had told how an American pilot, Bogard, and his friend, McGinnis, find a drunken English sailor (Claude Hope) trying to sleep in the middle of a Paris street.[2] Claude is doing this, he explains, because his boat is stored *under* the wharf at night, and he has nowhere else to go. Assuming that Claude is a shirker, Bogard and McGinnis take him up in their bomber to "show him some war." Claude proves to be a competent gunner, and congratulates the Americans for flying half the mission—and even landing—with an incompletely released bomb hanging from one of the wings. (The pilots, of course, had been unaware of the bomb.) Turnabout being fair play, Claude takes Bogard on his boat and shows *him* some war. The boat, manned by Claude and his friend (Ronnie Boyce-Smith), ejects torpedoes from its rear, then—with luck—gets out of their way. Bogard is impressed and has a case of Scotch delivered to Claude in the street; he tells the messenger to look for "a child

2. This description is excerpted from Bruce Kawin, *Faulkner and Film* (New York: Frederick Ungar Publishing Co., 1977), Chapter 4.

about six feet long." Later, Bogard reads that Claude and Ronnie have been lost in action, and himself makes a daring raid on an ammunition depot, then goes on to bomb the enemy's headquarters; his only regret is that "all the generals, the admirals, the presidents and the kings—theirs, ours, all of them" were not there to be destroyed. Faulkner's first screenplay, according to Hawks, followed this story exactly. Then Hawks went to show it to Irving Thalberg:

I said, "Close your door and start looking this over." He said, "Are you going to muddy it all up by changing it?" and I said, "No, I'm not going to muddy it up at all. I just want you to read it and see what a guy who doesn't know how to write scenarios [can do]." The next thing he came to me and said, "By the way, are you about getting ready to start?" And I said, "Yeah. I'll get Gary Cooper. I've got two kids, one called Bob Young and the other Franchot Tone. And we're all ready to go." And he said, "Well, you've got Joan Crawford, too"—she was the biggest star at that time. And I said, "You've got the wrong person," and he said, "Nope, we can't miss her—we haven't got a picture for Joan—we can't miss one, so you're stuck with it." Back to Bill, and I said, "Bill, we've got to put a girl in here," and he said, "Okay," and we made the picture and it wasn't a bad one at all.

One of the first laws of Hollywood is that creative autonomy is hard to come by; if there is a second law, it is that a serious *and* flexible artist can turn even such an arbitrary front-office demand as Thalberg's into usable material. Hawks continued:

What gummed up the story was when they told me Crawford was going to be in it. I used to go around with her when she first came out here. We're still very good friends. And they said, "By the way, Joan's down in the commissary waiting to talk to you." And I went down there and Joan said, "Is it true that there's no girl in your story?" Tears started to fall into her coffee cup, and I said, "Now,

look, I don't think you can get out of this. I don't think I can get out
of this. We both have contracts. You can make it absolutely misera-
ble unless you accept this well. And if you start taking it miserably,
those are the kind of scenes you're gonna make. I mean to tell you
now that I don't give a god damn what we do." Well, she promised
me—she would pin a flower in my lapel and give me a kiss each day
before we started work, and she was just great. But she read the
dialogue that the boys had—which was Faulkner's dialogue—and
she wanted [clipped] dialogue like that. And that subtracted from
[their] being, you know, so emotional. And also the clothes that she
wore—Jesus Christ! Well, that was the story. They lose a million
dollars if they don't have a [girl in the] thing, so Bill wrote the
script.

I've let Hawks tell you this story so that you can get some
sense of the working conditions at MGM in 1932–33, and perhaps some feel for Hawks and Crawford as people. Certainly
there is more of the factory than of the artist's colony evident
in this story, but there is also an atmosphere of friendship and
professionalism. If Faulkner ever became a resentful screenwriter, it was not in response to these conditions; he had legitimate grievances against the executives at Warner Brothers (remember Jack Warner's characterization of writers as "shmucks
with typewriters") and was in many situations a very nervous
man, but with Hawks he relaxed. They were good friends for
thirty years. Both enjoyed hunting, drinking, and telling stories; they even dressed in a similar manner (a fondness for comfortable tweeds) and often struck their co-workers as meticulous, stoic, and reserved. This tight-lipped privacy was the
main thing they had in common; no one in his right mind would
approach either man obsequiously or with nothing relevant to
say. Where their work was concerned, neither had any toler-
ance for wasted time or stupid orders, but each could do what
he had to. When Hawks abandoned *Battle Cry* after a budget
dispute, or stalked off the set of *Come and Get It* in mid-

shooting, it was not in petulance but with authority—the authority of a man who could demand, for instance, to see Jack Warner on the set, now. It is clear from his films—their classical economy, their fluid pace, their powerful tones, their sharp dialogue —that Hawks was a director and writer of great intelligence and skill; his works, after all, include *Scarface, Bringing Up Baby, Ball of Fire, I Was a Male War Bride, Red River, The Dawn Patrol, The Criminal Code, Twentieth Century, Only Angels Have Wings, His Girl Friday, Sergeant York, Monkey Business, Rio Bravo,* and of course *Today We Live, The Road to Glory, To Have and Have Not,* and *The Big Sleep.* Faulkner admired the way Hawks told a story; although his own writing was more experimental and intricate, he still recognized and respected the understated power, the fun, the seriousness of Hawks's methods, and experienced no professional crisis in writing for him. The basic difference between them was that Hawks preferred linear structures, while Faulkner was more interested in montage.

Thalberg's office wanted a girl in the picture, so Faulkner gave Ronnie Boyce-Smith a sister, Ann (or Diana, depending on the draft). This second draft, *Turn About* (finished in August, 1932), begins with one of those childhood-determines-the-rest-of-your-life scenes of which Faulkner was so fond.[3] Ronnie and Ann are playing in a muddy brook, accompanied by Claude—who, as a ward of the Boyce-Smith family, is essentially their brother. Ronnie tells Ann to go away from the water; when she refuses, he shoves her into the brook. Claude and Ronnie fight, but when Claude starts to win, Ann attacks him. A plane flies overhead, and they all stop fighting, enchanted. Ann says that when she grows up she will marry an aviator; Ronnie tells her that she is going to marry Claude. (The connections with the branch episode of *The Sound and the Fury*

3. *Ibid.*

are interesting, especially since the controlling brother in this story—Ronnie as a kind of Quentin—does have a "second self" his sister *can* marry. The theme of sublimated incest is general in Faulkner's work, but tends to find more positive expression in his screenplays than it does in the novels.) Later, when Ronnie goes off to school, he tells Claude to take care of Ann, since "girls have no sense." When Claude himself goes off to the same school, he passes her "care" on to Albert, the family servant, and tells Ann not to be a fool like most girls. Her marvelous retort is, "I'm not a fool. I never am." At school, Claude and Ronnie continue to play their favorite game of yelling "Beaver!" whenever they spot a bearded man; Ronnie is always ahead. (As adults, they call "Beaver" when they spot an enemy target with V-topped masts.)

Early in the war, their father dies in combat; the mother dies soon afterward. Now in their mid-teens, the three stand on a schoolground, listening to "a faint mutter of gunfire, as though heard from France." Ronnie and Claude promise to enlist together, when Claude (the younger) is of age. Remembering her parents, Ann exhorts the almost-brothers: "And then kill them! Kill them!"

At Oxford—in England—Ronnie and Ann meet Bogard. Ann takes an immediate dislike to him for "not being in khaki." Ronnie realizes that Ann curses Bogard too much and is probably attracted to him. Bogard falls in love with her and enlists, but when he goes to show off his uniform he finds that she and Ronnie have left for France; it is Claude's eighteenth birthday, and all three of them have joined up.

Bogard becomes an ace pilot. One night he finds Claude (whom he has never met) in the street; they go through most of the "turnabout" of the original story. By this time Claude and Ann have begun to sleep together; Claude has been drinking a great deal, out of his despair that the war will never end, that there will never be a way to go back to the normal world.

171

Ronnie is not censorious. When Bogard finally encounters and recognizes Ronnie, and goes to see Ann—angry that she has not saved herself for *him*—he calls her honesty (her not lying to him or to Ronnie) "filthy." Upset and furious, she shows him the door. The next day, Bogard goes out on the torpedo boat, and Claude is blinded. Claude tells Ann to marry Bogard and live a normal life; as a blind man, he says, he has no use for a wife. They have always been honest with each other about their not being in love, and Claude forces her not to start lying about it now. But when he insists that he *wants* her to go, Ann clutches him and says, "No! You're lying! Now you're lying!" (As is typical in Faulkner's screenplays—and fiction—the scene ends on this note of maximum tension.)

Ronnie learns that Bogard is to be assigned a virtual suicide mission: to bomb a heavily guarded cruiser that will otherwise interfere with a vital offensive. Bogard accepts the job, and there are several good scenes of the variously brave and cowardly reactions of his crew. When he hears the news, Claude insists that he and Ronnie torpedo the cruiser instead. They leave a note, passing on the "care" of Ann to Bogard. Bogard tries to stop them, but arrives too late; he and McGinnis fly to the battle site anyway. The torpedo mechanism jams, and Claude and Ronnie decide to ram the cruiser with their boat, torpedo and all. Just before they crash, Claude catches up with Ronnie in their game of "Beaver."

At this point Faulkner cuts, as he had in his original story, to the military dispatches that describe the climactic battle, and Bogard's going on to bomb the ammunition depot and enemy headquarters. (In the margin of the screenplay, Hawks wrote that the battle ought to be shown rather than described; this was the only place in the script Faulkner had allowed himself a literary montage in the style of Dos Passos.) The screenplay ends with Bogard and Ann, now married—as she had prophesied in childhood—placing a memorial to Ronnie and

Claude in the chapel of the town where they grew up. Bogard is angry with himself for not dying when they did (shades of *Sartoris*), but Ann insists that he did all he could. Faulkner retains the ending of his story, however, while still managing to work Ann into it:

BOGARD: Yes. God, God. If they had only all been there: generals, the admirals, the presidents, and the kings—theirs, ours, all of them! ANN: Hush. [Draws his head down to her breast, holding it there] Hush–hush.

Hawks was pleased with this script, as he had been with the first, but another problem came up. The child actors who were to play Ronnie, Ann, and Claude for the first quarter of the picture turned out to be unable to master British accents. By this time, Faulkner was in Mississippi, proofreading *Light in August*, so Hawks turned over the script to two professionals, Edith Fitzgerald and Dwight Taylor, instructing them to lengthen the battle scenes and write out the children. The screenwriters apparently found that without the childhood scenes the adolescent scenes made little sense, and decided to abandon the entire first half of the story. Faulkner tinkered with this third and final version, by now called *Today We Live*, adding two important scenes that salvaged some of the echoes of *The Sound and the Fury* (the "say it again" scene between Ronnie and Ann, which is a healthy—and I think deliberate—contrast to the "say it again"/"Dalton Ames" exchange in Quentin's chapter; and the "voice that breathed o'er Eden" speech that Claude delivers to Ronnie).

There is no question but that *Turn About*, the second screenplay, is superior both to the original story and to the finished film. One interesting thing that the story and the film share is terribly clipped dialogue. In the second version, the dialogue tends to be more natural and resonant. My guess is

173

that Fitzgerald and Taylor went back to the story for help in revising that second script, and that they are responsible for some of the staccato dialogue in *Today We Live*; in any case it is evident that Faulkner revised *their* version just before or during shooting, so he probably liked what they did. (He said in a letter written after he had finished the second version that he "would have made this script for nothing, being interested in the story."[4]) If, when you see *Today We Live*, you fill in the childhood histories I've outlined and imagine that you're watching the continuation of that story, you'll have a fair idea of how Faulkner intended "Turn About" to look on the screen.

Late in 1932 or early in 1933 Faulkner and Hawks went to see a picture called *Secrets*; Faulkner didn't like it. "You make me mad, for goodness sake," said Hawks. "A ghost story is really a *good story* and this is beautifully told." So, says Hawks, Faulkner "went off and wrote a ghost story." It wasn't quite that simple, since what Faulkner did was to adapt a wartime diary MGM had been assigning to various writers for many years, *War Birds*. Thanks to Hawks's input, he changed it to a ghost story of sorts—Hawks called it a "ghosts from the past" story—perhaps after his own version had already started to take shape without the ghost element. He also substituted Bayard and John Sartoris for the original hero, threw in both "Ad Astra" and "All the Dead Pilots," and gave *Sartoris* (after the fact) a different ending, thematically anticipating "An Odor of Verbena" (*War Birds* lets Bayard forgive both himself and Johnny's killers, and survive). So at this stage of his career Faulkner was quite definitely using film-writing to advance his own thinking, to try out versions of his stories, and to gain a large audience for his own work.

In 1934 Faulkner began work on *Absalom, Absalom!* under

---

4. Joseph Blotner, *Selected Letters of William Faulkner* (New York: Random House, 1977), 66.

BRUCE KAWIN

the title *Dark House*. He took a break to work on *Sutter's Gold* for Hawks at Universal; it seems evident from what I can manage to deciper (all that's left is a badly scratched microfilm of what looks like a fuzzy carbon) that Faulkner worked from Eisenstein's 1930 treatment of the property, toning down both the montage and the politics, and pointing up the story of a man obsessed first with gold and then with justice. Before doing *Sutter's Gold*, Faulkner described *Dark House* as the story of "a man who outraged the land, and the land then turned and destroyed the man's family." One month after *Sutter* he described what he now called *Absalom, Absalom!* as the story of "a man who wanted a son through pride, and got too many of them and they destroyed him."[5] My guess is that he got the first theme out of his system with *Sutter's Gold* and thereby improved the novel.

*Absalom* gave Faulkner much trouble in the writing. At one point he asked Hawks for advice—or else Hawks just volunteered it:

I got mad at him one day and I said, "Stop writing about these god damned hillbillies that you know down there." "Who should I write about?" And I said, "Well, you ought to know about people *flying*." "Oh yeah," he said, "I know—two men and a girl—the girl and one of the men were wing-walkers and the other was the pilot. She was pregnant and she didn't know which one." I said, "That's a good story. Write it." So he wrote *Pylon*, through the eyes of a drunken reporter—who was Bill, himself. I didn't want to make it into a movie or anything. I didn't tell him that.

This conversation seems to be the link between the story "Honor" and the novel *Pylon*. In any case, *Pylon* bled off some of the incoherent and frenzied energy that might have ruined *Absalom*. In the process he abandoned a minor project, "A

5. *Ibid.*, 78, 84.

175

Child's Garden of Motion Picture Scripts," which was to have been a parodistic send-up of the genre. It is relevant that at one point he told Hawks, "I have no qualms at all about stealing from you; I think it's good stuff." As I read their relationship, there was no place in it for Faulkner to lie to Hawks; I think that their mutual respect was genuine, and that Faulkner's grousing about Hollywood in his letters, which was also probably genuine, was simply part of an ambivalence and not the whole story. I think that Hawks didn't tell Faulkner he wouldn't want to film *Pylon* simply because he wanted his friend to get over his *Absalom* block and get the easier story written. It's also worth noting that Hawks considered *Pylon* "one of the least valuable of his novels" and was not, in telling me this story, trying to take credit for influencing Faulkner.

He was still working on *Absalom* when he collaborated with Joel Sayre on the script for *The Road to Glory*. It is what Hawks would have called a "two men and a girl" story. The setting is "1916, Somewhere in France," which is to say: in the middle of the war, in the middle of nowhere, on the road to something that might as well be called glory. It is an existential story about the feel of the limbo in which history repeats itself, and it is held together by three repetitions of a speech made by a series of commanders to a series of men: the personnel changes, but the regiment continues, and every trip to the front lines is in its own way the first trip. (If it sounds as if I'm reading-in Mircea Eliade's *Myth of the Eternal Return*, which was written later, please note that Captain LaRoche [Warner Baxter], the commander who delivers the first two of these speeches and who is replaced by Lieutenant Denet [Fredric March], who delivers the third speech, reassures his lover that he'll come back from the front because he always does, because he's eternal; in any case, the renewing force of repetition is part of Faulkner's own metaphysics of history.) At the beginning of the story, Denet joins LaRoche's company; Faulkner

176

had him enter in a glass-walled hearse, drunk, but that scene was cut in the later drafts and Faulkner did not restore it when he helped Hawks put together the shooting version. LaRoche, who deals with the strain of command by downing great amounts of cognac and aspirin, is in love with a nurse, Monique [June Lang]. He gives her a rosary that had been given to him by his sister, whom he loved very much, and asks her to keep it for him against his return. (This rosary, by the way, was thought up by the producer, Darryl Zanuck, but there are comparable props with much the same purpose in Faulkner's draft. The sister idea was Faulkner's and was probably added while he was on the set.) Soon Denet meets Monique during an air raid. When the men go to the front they contend with a number of problems, notably that their trench is being mined from beneath by the Germans. They make it back safely, and the relationship between Denet and Monique deepens until they feel they have to break it off for LaRoche's sake. The next time the company moves up, LaRoche's father [Lionel Barrymore] is with them. When they come back this time, Denet is wounded, LaRoche is blind, and the love affair is confirmed. LaRoche then goes on a suicide mission, guided by his father. Denet takes over the command; when last seen he makes LaRoche's speech, tosses down a handful of aspirin, and is clearly with Monique. One is tempted to say that LaRoche *has* returned, but as Denet—that there is a definite cyclical force at work.

The connections with *Today We Live* are manifold. Blindness is a major threat in both films (as it is in *Soldiers' Pay*, which may have been one of the reasons Hawks—who always considered blindness to be prime dramatic material—found the novel interesting in the first place); it also turns up in *Land of the Pharaohs*. In both films the blinded lover goes on a suicide mission so that the woman he has slept with can be with the man she really loves. Both of those missions involve being the victim of one's own weapon—the unlaunched torpedo in *Today*

*We Live*, and the bombardments that must be directed from the target area in *The Road to Glory*. The treatment of the themes of heroism, suicide, blindness, and love-conflict is consistent in both films, with the difference that *The Road to Glory* has more existential force and *Today We Live* more emphasis on sublimated incest. The link between Paul LaRoche and Claude Hope is Quentin Compson, who killed himself because he could neither possess his sister sexually, nor want to—whose love turned to a longing for death. *Today We Live* and *The Road to Glory* are more a diptych than a double feature, very much like *The Sound and the Fury* and *Absalom, Absalom!*, both intra- and infra-structurally. This should not be surprising, since *The Road to Glory* was written while *Absalom* was being finished, and since *Today We Live* examines the perils of innocence in a waste land in terms borrowed both from the Sartoris stories and from the Quentin chapter of *The Sound and the Fury*. Several of Hawks's major themes are in evidence too: the love between two men (Claude and Ronnie, LaRoche and Denet), the importance of professionalism, the isolating force of blindness, the attractiveness of frank and powerful women, and an acceptance of sexual maturity. Hawks was an optimist who could always see the dark side—a man who was most comfortable planning a comedy in the morning and going to the races in the afternoon, but whose jokes almost always dance above an existential abyss (into which they do not usually fall, and that's the essential pleasure of his films). Besides being the most well-read director of his generation—the first producer to adapt Conrad, for instance, and the close friend of Hemingway and Faulkner—Hawks was something very rare in the film industry: a grown-up. One final point about the similarity between these two films: Hawks felt that he was allowed to repeat himself and that most artists do so all the time. The times he most consistently called Faulkner for help were those when he wanted to adapt something from an earlier film; he particularly admired Faulkner's versatility at making repetition fresh.

The rest of the work Faulkner did at 20th Century-Fox ranges from the colorfully competent (his treatment for *Drums Along the Mohawk*) to the awful (*Submarine Patrol*). He wrote some beautiful dialogue for *Banjo on My Knee*, but it was considered too long-winded and not used at all. His *Slave Ship* was a good script, but I haven't seen the picture and don't know how much of it reached the screen. He put in some time on *Gunga Din* at RKO, most of it spent trying to convince his fellow-writers that Din was a black and needed to be characterized in such terms (one might have thought Sam Jaffe had enough trouble with the role already!); apparently he lost that argument.

In 1942 Faulkner started to work at Warner Brothers, a studio that exploited him unconscionably. He did some of his best film-writing on scripts that were never used, so that his name is associated with a minor film like *Stallion Road* although that film was shot from Longstreet's script, which Longstreet himself admitted was inferior to Faulkner's earlier draft. There is a body of good, unproduced, and single-authored work: *Country Lawyer, Stallion Road, Fog over London*, and *The DeGaulle Story*. There are his major contributions to *The Big Sleep* and *To Have and Have Not*. There is his section of Hawks's unproduced *Battle Cry*. There are his minor but effective contributions to *Air Force* and *Mildred Pierce*. Then there was his moonlighting work on Jean Renoir's classic, *The Southerner*. And there's the garbage, the real wasted time: *Escape in the Desert* and *Northern Pursuit*. Working on his own during this period he also wrote two very interesting scripts: a really brilliant vampire film called *Dreadful Hollow*, and a ludicrous, awful adaptation of *Absalom* called *Revolt in the Earth*.

The screenplays written during the forties that show best just how good Faulkner was at his business and how fundamentally the themes of his fiction are expressed are *Dreadful Hollow*, which was never filmed, and his half of *The Big Sleep*, whose most complex and disturbing scenes were deleted before shooting began. The produced film that has the most adequate Faulkner "feel" to it is *The Southerner*, but no one knows how much of it he wrote. And the produced film from this period that has, scene for scene and structure for structure, the most of Faulkner's actual writing in it turns out to be *To Have and Have Not*. Most of those departures from Hemingway's novel that have so bothered litterateurs were in fact dreamed up by Faulkner—not Hawks—after Warner gave in to government pressure against a film about rum-running in Cuba; it was Faulkner who thought of switching the location to Martinique, who condensed the figure of "Slim" out of two women in the previous screenplays (by Jules Furthman), and who was most interested in the anti-Vichy elements of the new story. Most of the time, in fact, Faulkner was writing only one day ahead of the shooting, and although that didn't stop Hawks from revising most of the dialogue into rhythms that were more natural for the actors (revisions and deletions that apparently did not bother Faulkner), it did insure Faulkner's position as head author; no one was about to throw away his script, especially since Faulkner was saving the studio a tremendous amount of money by making it possible for them to film a project that would otherwise have had to be abandoned halfway through production.

After *Dreadful Hollow* Faulkner worked on only three films worth mentioning. He looked over and partially revised Ben Maddow's script for *Intruder in the Dust*. He wrote a screenplay for Hawks from *The Left Hand of God*, but Hawks abandoned the project when a priest advised him (probably after seeing Faulkner's script, but there's no way to know) that the picture would alienate Catholic audiences. And he collaborated on *Land of the Pharaohs*, a forgettable but entertaining spectacle which Hawks has struck from the list of his works. Hawks had started out as an engineer, and he and Faulkner had a good time inventing a system of sand hydraulics to seal the pyramid and a ramp for the stones; they were even complimented on their ideas by a group of archaeologists who were digging in the vicinity. One reason the picture bombed is that Hawks gave Faulkner license to invent a genuinely destructive and deceitful woman; he did such a powerful job of it that none of the good guys who were supposed to balance the picture had dramatic force. Faulkner saw the picture as a remake of *Red River*, but Hawks had wanted him on the picture because of the religious angle, particularly the discrepancy between life as it was lived and death as it was planned.

When I asked Hawks to sum up their relationship, he said: "Well, I got help whenever I wanted it from Faulkner. And I never knew him to miss. Just when I thought that I was going wrong, you know, I'd have a scene where I didn't know what the hell to do, I got a good answer from him. I got help in writing, and we were damned good friends, and we had fun together, you know."

That's the story, and I hope you enjoy the films.

# Faulkner
# and the Avant-Garde

HUGH KENNER

Faulkner is clearly part of something modern: we have no difficulty thinking of whole pages and chapters of *The Sound and the Fury* or *Absalom, Absalom!* which it is inconceivable that anyone could have written before the complex revolution of verbal and narrative techniques we associate with the early twentieth century. Yet avant-garde is a metaphor of which we sense the wrongness as soon as we apply it. It is a military metaphor; the avant-garde is the forward edge of an army, or perhaps a scouting party, or a clutch of purposeful dynamiters —in any case a coherent group under discipline. Applied to the arts, this metaphor reflects a bourgeois fear of being plotted against, and a plot entails a group. Faulkner wasn't a group man. No other major twentieth-century writer was so isolated from his peers. The list of men he admired but never met would astonish by its length. In Paris, in 1925, he seems to have glimpsed Joyce once, at a cafe. They did not meet; nor did Faulkner meet Pound, nor Hemingway, nor Gertrude Stein, nor even Sylvia Beach.

Poets, it may be, congregate more than novelists, perhaps because, putting fewer words on fewer pages, they have more time to spare from driving the pen. Though Joyce seems to have met nearly everybody, it was because they sought him out, during the nearly twenty years he lived in Paris, and revolutionaries of the word had more reasons for coming to Paris

than to Oxford, Mississippi. Still, allowing for the fact that professional gregariousness has not been a conspicuous trait of
novelists, there is something idiosyncratic about Faulkner's
isolation. He did not even talk much about his reading—his
equivocation about his knowledge of *Ulysses* is famous—and
when, in late years, confronting undergraduate audiences, he
was asked about his peers he tended to answer in lists: "Wolfe,
John Dos Passos, Hemingway, Willa Cather, John Steinbeck"
ran one such list; and as for detailed comment, he would merely rank them according to what he called "the splendor of the
failure": that ranking ran "Wolfe, Faulkner, Dos Passos, Hemingway and Steinbeck."[1]

Such evasiveness seems meant to create a presumption:
that the heart of writing is ultimately moral, that each writer
confronts his aspiration and his failure alone, and that what
writers learn from one another is either private or trivial. But
avant-garde by definition professes a community of aim. It is
held together by what its members profess in common, by in-
terchange, by an emphasis on the part of the craft that is
learned, shared, exchanged, sharpened in the phrasing and the
exchanging. Manifestoes are its staple, and cafe talk; and if
Joyce for example signed no manifestoes, he is nonetheless
legitimately claimed by a modernism that learned from his
example, in part because he had so clearly thought out his
methods that his example could teach them, and teach the
attitudes behind them.

Faulkner clearly wanted no part of pedagogy, nor of literary politics. But in talking as he did about the intensities of
solitary aspiration and failure, he seemed to disavow the other
face of avant-gardism as well, its emphasis on what can be defined as a community of aim and means: the deliberate craft,

---

1. Joseph Blotner, *Faulkner: A Biography* (New York: Random House,
1974), II, 1232.

the statable grounds of self-criticism. Faulkner, it seems, did not mind anyone's believing that the hard work he did came from his gut: that there was nothing to talk about save the sense of dedicated effort.

This proposition may be conveniently illustrated from the history of one twentieth-century group, the imagists, who were united, insofar as anything united them save mutual acquaintance, by a program with three points: (1) "Direct treatment of the 'thing,' whether subjective or objective"; (2) no unnecessary word; (3) a metric obeying the phrase rather than the metronome. We may think of this program under either of two aspects, the public and the technical. One part of its intent—and the purpose of publishing it rather than confining it to talk and private circulation—was pedagogic: to alter public taste, to define criteria that will exclude much that gets readily admired, and focus attention on much that gets forgotten, or admired without perception. For it does not describe only future poems: it isolates certain past ones. Sappho meets these criteria; so does Catullus; so does Villon. Swinburne does not, running riot with unnecessary words; and if many Greek writers were, as Pound said, "rather Swinburnian," the effect of the imagist canon is to isolate Sappho and the epigrammatists of the Greek anthology from what is inertly celebrated as "Greek Literature." So a manifesto that seems phrased for the use of poets can alter the perceptions of a reader of poetry who has no ambition to write a line.

The other aspect of the program is technical; it gives a poet criteria for revision. Have I worked for direct presentation, or contented myself with abstraction? Have I admitted nonfunctioning words, words maybe that swarm out of habit, or that fill out a rhythm and do nothing else? Have I permitted my rhythm to sway mechanically?

We may add that in redefining a tradition, and in isolating technical matters from it, the imagist canon allowed poets to admire Sappho or Catullus, and aspire to emulate their excellence, without imitating them directly, thus saving young writers much time they might otherwise lose executing pastiche. In this respect it defines prose canons too; Stendhal for instance is by extension an imagist, Stendhal who based his style, he said, on that of the *Code Napoleon*. So is Jane Austen, so is the Joyce of *Dubliners*, but not Dickens, nor Walter Scott.

Now clearly William Faulkner would not have subscribed to this particular set of criteria, beyond perhaps agreeing, through a cloud of pipe smoke, that in some ways what was proposed was a pretty good thing. The famous description of Popeye in the opening paragraphs of *Sanctuary* might pass for the writing of a writer of imagist prose: "His face had a queer, bloodless color, as though seen by electric light; against the sunny silence, in his slanted straw hat and his slightly akimbo arms, he had that vicious depthless quality of stamped tin." "Sunny silence" looks like a mannered synaesthesia, but "sunny" is needed to offset "electric light": under the sky, this face is unnatural in color. And the superb "stamped tin," with its clanked dull rhythm—how much contempt resonates in the sound of the words, a "musical phrase" indeed if we eschew the sentimental connotations of "musical," to reinforce the absolute finality of the image. Still, no manifesto would have made Faulkner forego his love of many words, superfluous if we examine them one by one but defensible as contributing to a copiousness, a garrulousness, a quality of psychic overflowing he discerned in the tradition of oral storytelling and prized above any satisfactions to be obtained from erasure, paring, spareness.

But the real point is not an incompatibility between Faulkner's practice and any particular set of modernist criteria. The real point is that he had no special use for either of the two aspects of any program. He had no special ambition to reform public taste, none of the pedagogical fervor of the born avant-

185

gardist. And he had no desire, by any commitment now, to limit the scope of his operations in the future.

We have already glanced at one reason for this temperamental aversion. The base of Faulkner's storytelling was oral, and every twentieth-century avant-garde movement one can think of was dedicated to canons not oral but literary, canons which if they admit copiousness require even it to seem a little synthetic, like the lists in *Ulysses*, every item of which Joyce means us to feel can be justified on deliberated and specifiable grounds. The assumption that we are free to weigh and question every word is an assumption peculiar to written literature, where the words stay still for inspection as they do not when someone is talking; to written literature, moreover, which has accepted and come to terms with its status as writing, in fact as writing for a printing press, and envisions a reader silent before printed pages. In this sense the entire thrust of twentieth-century modernism—the Revolution of the Word which commenced in English about 1910, inheriting French developments that date from 1880 and before; the complex eponymous movement that gave us *Ulysses*, *The Waste Land*, the *Cantos*, the *Paterson* of Williams, and the poems of Marianne Moore—its thrust was toward a consolidation of all that printed paper implies: the well-wrought artifact, the tireless revision, the skilled reader, the habitual rereader, in an economy of typescripts, numbered pages, typographic cues for which a speaking voice has no equivalent, etymologies, dictionaries. (Shakespeare had no dictionary.) Questioned about his relationship to this context of creativity, questioned moreover by questioners in classrooms who had no idea that any other context was pertinent, Faulkner was understandably either brusque or evasively polite, feeling perhaps like a shaman who has wandered into a conference of brain surgeons, knowing that he commands skills of incantation incompatible with their discourse of subtle instruments.

A narrative passage from *The Hamlet* runs like this:

And after that, not nothing to do until morning except to stay close enough where Henry can call her until it's light enough to chop the wood to cook breakfast and then help Mrs. Littlejohn wash the dishes and make the beds and sweep while watching the road. Because likely any time now Flem Snopes will get back from wherever he has been since the auction, which of course is to town naturally to see about his cousin that's got into a little legal trouble and so get that five dollars. 'Only maybe he won't give it back to me,' she says, and maybe that's what Mrs. Littlejohn thought too, because she never said nothing.

Though written, this is not *writing*, not by the criteria Stendhal taught us, or Flaubert, or Conrad, or Joyce. Not merely are its sentence rhythms those of oral narrative (rhythms Conrad eschewed despite his fondness for oral narrators; rhythms Joyce in synthesizing them beautifully in "Cyclops" nevertheless interrupted thirty-two times with interpolations from the domain of print): not only that, but it requires the reader to play the role of hearer, participating in the "now" of "any time now" and in the speculation about where Flem had been. Not the sentence rhythms but the role forced on the reader will serve to discriminate what is radically written from what is radically oral. The reader-as-listener must pretend as listeners do that he does not confront anonymously the anonymity of print, that he is acquainted with time and place and genealogy, that he knows people who are barely named, that characters and their pasts need not be cunningly "introduced" because knowledge of all that attaches to a name is part of the communal stock the reader shares with a community which includes the storyteller and of which the bounds are indefinite.

This is of course a radically unreal supposition, but we brave it out and pick up such knowledge the way a tactful stranger does, never impeding nor embarrassing the storyteller.

187

We pick it up from clues, which means close reading: which means, since reading despite the oral convention is what we are after all doing, that we approach the Faulkner text very like New Critics, as if it had been written by James Joyce. Hence a curious strain at the heart of anyone's confrontation with a Faulkner novel. For ideal comprehension we must take notes, turn back to an earlier page, keep track of time schemes and family trees; we must simultaneously pretend that we need do none of this, need only listen to a voice we ourselves supply. The puzzle we are put to, making out what really did happen, is exactly the trouble we incur with a difficult written text in which the paring away of unnecessary words has been carried perhaps excessively far.

What Faulkner tended to pare away, or perhaps didn't think of supplying in the first place, isn't the verbiage which both imagism and the more general canons of international modernism have interdicted, but information, the sort of information a storyteller's hearers take for granted because they are part of his community. Take, for a brief and amusing illustration, the story "An Error in Chemistry," an unimportant pot-boiler nine editors rejected before *Ellery Queen's Mystery Magazine* paid $300 for it in 1945. The story turns on a mystery writer's gimmick: an impostor exposes himself by not knowing how a Mississippian would make a cold toddy. He spoons sugar into raw whiskey, which won't dissolve it, instead of into water to which the whiskey will then be added, and everybody in the room is aghast at this violation not only of chemistry but of an immutable folkway. As the narrator tells us, "I had not only watched Uncle Gavin, and the sheriff when he would come to play chess with Uncle Gavin, but Uncle Gavin's father too who was my grandfather, and my own father before he died, and all the other men who would come to Grandfather's house who drank cold toddies": that is how you acquire that sort of information; any member of the storyteller's community has acquired it likewise; the northern impostor hasn't. And in the first version of the story, the one his agent tried in vain to place for five years, Faulkner apparently forgot that most of his readers would be in the position of the northern impostor: failed at the very climax of his tale to specify what error the impostor made: forgot in short to tell us outlanders what any Mississippian would know.[2] The incident illuminates his principle of omission, which isn't that of a disciplined imagist at all.

So he makes the modernist demand that we read slowly and closely for reasons diametrically opposite to those that govern modernist orthodoxy. The modernist assumption, arising from the economy of print, is that to tell your story, secure your effect, there exists a discoverable combination of just the right words, a minimal set of words, not to be exceeded, and to be arranged in exactly the right order. The James Joyce of a famous anecdote spent all day on two sentences, not seeking the exact word—he had his words already—but seeking the perfect order of fifteen words in two sentences. "There is an order in every way appropriate. I think I have it."[3] But the storyteller confronting a living audience hasn't time for that order of research; if he began to fumble over two sentences he would rapidly lose his audience. He is apt to tell his story over and over again, never twice in quite the same way. His unit of attention is not the word but the event, and the practice that shapes the tale toward its definitive ordering is likely to experiment as Faulkner often did, rearranging whole blocks of narrative, placing this incident now before, now after that one, until the most satisfying version is certified by communal agreement and embedded in his repertoire. But even the "final" version will not be told twice in quite the same words.

2. Blotner, *Faulkner*, II, 1189n.
3. Frank Budgen, *James Joyce and the Making of Ulysses*, 20.

Being engaged with his audience, the storyteller (or the bardic singer of tales) is little tempted to be engaged with himself. Walter Ong, our prime theorist of these matters, remarks that "You cannot find Homer's personality in the *Iliad*, although you might find the personality of an entire culture there."[4] Nor can you find Faulkner's personality in *Light in August*—not because, like Joyce, he took conscious steps to keep it out, playing "the God of creation, . . . within or behind or beyond or above his handiwork, invisible, refined out of existence, indifferent, paring his fingernails," but because his absorption with tale and audience make it unlikely that self-consciousness will creep in. It is the writer who is conscious of being alone with a sheet of paper, making word-by-word decisions and revisions, hesitating all day over two sentences, who is apt to find a self-absorption invading his work unless he makes deliberate resolves to keep it out.

Faulkner's oral storytelling mode, it is commonplace to observe, is that of a provincial culture with its small towns, its agriculture, its still living religion, its implicit norms of conduct. Drawing an analogy between Faulkner and Yeats, Cleanth Brooks has quoted the Irishman Sean O'Faolain, who thought that life in Mississippi sounded very like life in County Cork:

There is the same passionate provincialism; the same local patriotism; the same southern nationalism—those long explicit speeches of Gavin Stevens in *Intruder in the Dust* might, *mutatis mutandis*, be uttered by a southern Irishman—the same feeling that whatever happens in Ballydehob or in Jefferson has never happened anywhere else before, and is more important than anything that happened in any period of history in any part of the cosmos; there is the same vanity of an old race; the same gnawing sense of old defeat; the same capacity for intense hatred; a good deal of the same harsh folk-humor; the same acidity; the same oscillation between un-

4. Walter J. Ong, *Interfaces of the Word* (Ithaca, New York: Cornell University Press, 1977), 221.

bounded self-confidence and total despair; the same escape through sport and drink.[5]

We may next note that of the two great writers born in nineteenth-century Ireland, the elder, W. B. Yeats, was excited by collections of folk narratives and even helped Lady Gregory collect them, while the younger, James Joyce, affected a bored contempt for such materials though he put them to covert use in *Finnegans Wake*. Yeats (who like Faulkner went on to win the Nobel Prize, bestowed by a committee with a demonstrable predilection for regional writers) argued memorably that

> All that we did, all that we said or sang
> Must come from contact with the soil, from that
> Contact everything Antaeus-like grew strong.

Joyce (whom the Nobel committee overlooked, omitting as it did so to honor the greatest man of letters of the twentieth century) called Ireland "the afterthought of Europe" and spent his last decades in Europe's most cosmopolitan capital, Paris.

One cannot imagine modern letters without Joyce; one cannot imagine modern Ireland without Yeats. To say that is not to confine the interest of Yeats to the Irish; without Yeats we should all be deprived of a memorable, an irreplaceable body of work. (Many curricula moreover would be impoverished, so great is his pedagogical usefulness.) But it is difficult to specify the difference Yeats made to any other major writer, whatever moral difference his existence assuredly made to the next generation in Ireland; whereas Joyce was so great an innovator his mark is on all prose narrative since the publication of *Ulysses*.

In making this distinction we are preparing for a clarification of twentieth-century modernism which in turn will help

5. Sean O'Faolain, *The Vanishing Hero*, as quoted in Cleanth Brooks, *William Faulkner: The Yoknapatawpha Country* (New Haven: Yale University Press, 1963), 2.

clarify Faulkner's relationship to it. One way of describing what happened to English in the twentieth century is this: English ceased to be the language of a country and its former colonies; it became instead simply an available language, regarded differently by writers in England, in the United States, in Ireland. Three regional literatures arose: the English, the American, the Irish, writers in each country bringing different social assumptions to their common dictionary. Take the word "accurate." An Englishman, guided by the Latin *cura*, "care," in an etymology he may not even know, feels *trouble* in accuracy; it is achieved by taking care. William Carlos Williams said of something he was writing, "As far as I have gone it is accurate": "it," not "I"; the emphasis is not on the trouble but on the close tolerances of the result. An American senses in accuracy a technological *precision*. James Joyce in *Ulysses* presents Mr. Philip Beaufoy "in accurate morning dress"; we may be tempted to say that an Englishman who invokes accuracy is being troubled, an American is being precise, and an Irishman is being funny. Such examples could be multiplied by the thousand. James Joyce wrote of an English priest, "How different are the words *home, Christ, ale, master*, on his lips and on mine! . . . His language, so familiar and so foreign, will always be for me an acquired speech." Yet Joyce had grown up speaking no language save what everyone called "English."

Three languages then, drawn from the same dictionary; three social experiences likewise; and by the mid-twentieth century, for the first time, three literatures. Earlier Irish writers had won their fame in England, earlier American ones had hoped to. We may speak now of the literatures of the three provinces, England too a province like the others. For the twentieth century also gave birth to a fourth English, that of international modernism.

It seems clear, for instance, that *Ulysses* is in no meaningful way a part of Irish literature; nor is *Waiting for Godot* (which is not part of French literature either, though the first version was written, by an Irishman, in French). Is *The Waste Land* part of English literature? Probably not; not the way *The Vanity of Human Wishes* is, or *Mrs. Dalloway*. It is easier to assign these works, and others, to a new international tradition, the language of which is to be found in an English dictionary; much as it is easier to assign the oeuvre of Picasso to something analogously international than to the history of Spanish art, or the history of French. Virginia Woolf's work on the other hand, despite certain avant-garde mannerisms, is simply English; Sean O'Casey's is Irish; Ernest Hemingway's is American; and so is Scott Fitzgerald's and most of Faulkner's.

Such a taxonomy is not a means of assigning value but a way of assessing relationships. The masters of international modernism were the century's great innovators, on whose innovations the writers of the three provinces habitually drew. They pay for their grandeur, though, with a certain abstractness—an attentuation of the richness and power that is available to a novelist or poet who is working within a culture, with the culture's norms and its minute signals. Little that is specifically Irish, except the precision of speech rhythm and a taste for the comedy of logic, has survived the process by which Samuel Beckett's novels and plays were extracted from the language he learned in Dublin. Joyce bent his intention not on being Irish but on being a pupil of the Jesuits who chanced to have grown up in Ireland. But remove his southernness from Faulkner, or remove Sligo and the Anglo-Irish pride from Yeats, and nothing much is left.

We have in Faulkner, then, a distinguished and powerful instance of the sort of local literary tradition the modernism of the twentieth century has made possible: a way of being intensely local which profits from a range of expressive devices not local at all but developed by several great contemporary innovators whose intention was to see their native region from afar, with cosmopolitan eyes. Joyce could not have written in Dublin, nor Eliot in St. Louis, nor Pound in either Idaho (where he was born) or Pennsylvania (where he grew up). They went to the great capitals, never forgetting their roots, always looking back.

But Faulkner could not have written *The Sound and the Fury* in Paris, nor could William Carlos Williams have carried his Jersey materials there. And yet every page of theirs bespeaks their contemporaneity with Joyce and with Pound, but for whom neither could have written as he did.

We may want to ask, finally, what all this implies about Faulkner's reader. We have employed, for expository convenience, the model of the communal storyteller, who tells tall tales, tales his hearers already half know, and tells them over and over, he and those who hear knit in a web of comprehension a great deal of which need not even entail what is spoken. Such a man enjoys extraordinary intimacy with the hearers he knows, and may be half-incomprehensible fifty miles away, where certain names have no potency.

Moving such a model from folklorists' Platonism toward reality, we obtain for instance Faulkner's V. K. Ratliff, with his perfect assurance of how to enter a store "on the gallery of which apparently the same men who had been there when he saw it last a year ago were still sitting," and his sense of how to obtain an audience by dropping the impenetrable phrase "Goat-rancher." People who feign indifference to Ratliff's presence absorb every word he says, as a story perfectly shaped to pique curiosity winds from a teasing opener to a climax that restates the opening in new light. He is like the bard Demodokos in the *Odyssey*, a portrait within the work of the shaper of the work itself.

But this too is Platonized. Demodokos may give us Homer's sense of himself, but Faulkner, a man in a study with a pen, is no V. K. Ratliff, nor do his readers sit on the gallery of even an ideal store. Faulkner's fame did not start in Oxford and spread outward. It started in places like Paris and New York, and eventually reached Mississippi. "Mr. Faulkner a great writer?" ran an Oxford comment on the 1939 cover story in *Time*; "Well, they sure wouldn't hire him to write a Chamber of Commerce booklet for the town."[6]

Print is perilous stuff, like electricity. They read print as far away as New York, and stories should be kept in the family. And Dublin, by the way, contains dozens of raconteurs who will tell you that the city contained and still contains a host of storytellers more gifted than Joyce. As it may; he was more than a storyteller. And they say his great gift was for taking in Americans.

No, the ideal Faulkner reader is not the ideal listener the communal storyteller supposes. Nor is he that "ideal reader suffering from an ideal insomnia" whom Joyce presupposed and did so much to train: the patient correlator of clues and looker-up of stray facts. The ideal Faulkner reader must combine New-Critical skills of textual response with an imaginative flexibility that can bend salmon-supple in and out of the Yoknapatawpha community: for if you read him as if he were Joyce you are repeatedly snagged by what seem like hundreds of running feet of lazily coiled rusty rhetoric and thickets of unregarded narrative gestures, whereas if you read him as if he were a comfortable old-fashioned novelist the coinages, the neologisms, the inner monologues and resonant italics—all the contrivances of literary technology—betray you. And if you read him as if he were an awkward amalgam of both you get no satisfaction at all. It is a unique role that the reader must play, seeing folk material imitated, synthesized, by the devices of the twentieth-century avant-garde, being aware that that is what is going on and yet responding as if he were what he can-

6. Blotner, *Faulkner*, II, 1016.

not be, a sympathetic member of a vanished community. Our role demands tact and resourcefulness, an ability to adjust repeatedly to altered focus, and we may be years learning it. The avant-garde created Faulkner's techniques but did not train his reader. We must acquire our training from his books.

# Contributors

MALCOLM COWLEY is a poet, critic, essayist, editor, literary historian, and translator. Book editor of *The New Republic* for many years, Cowley is perhaps best known for *Exile's Return*, his memoir of literary life in Paris and New York during the 1920s and 1930s, and for the Viking *Portable Faulkner*, which he edited and for which he wrote a memorable introduction. In his *Faulkner-Cowley File*, a collection of letters and reminiscences, Cowley recounts the publication of the Viking *Portable*, which revived interest in William Faulkner in the 1940s when his books were virtually out of print. Cowley's latest book is *—And I Worked at the Writer's Trade: Chapters of Literary History, 1918–1978*.

HORTON FOOTE is a dramatist, screen and television writer, and novelist. In addition to writing numerous original plays for stage and television, Foote has transferred stories from one medium to another, writing the book for the musical *Gone with the Wind*, from the novel by Margaret Mitchell; creating an award-winning script for the film version of Harper Lee's novel *To Kill a Mockingbird*; and rewriting *The Chase*, his own play, as a novel. Among Foote's adaptations of William Faulkner's works are *The Old Man* and *Tomorrow* for motion pictures. He recently adapted Faulkner's "Barn Burning" for the PBS series *Short Story in America*.

# Contributors

BRUCE KAWIN is a poet as well as a specialist in film history and contemporary British and American fiction. Associate professor of English at the University of Colorado, Kawin has been Lecturer in English and Film at the University of California, Riverside, and Specialist in Film Analysis for the American Film Institute. His books include *Telling It Again and Again: Repetition in Literature and Film*; *Faulkner and Film*; and *Mindscreen: Bergman, Godard, and the Language of First-Person Film*. Kawin has also written "A Faulkner Filmography" and book and film reviews for *Film Quarterly* and *Take One*.

HUGH KENNER has for many years taught at Johns Hopkins University. In 1975 he was named Andrew W. Mellon Professor in Humanities at that institution. He has received two fellowships from the Guggenheim Foundation and has been a visiting professor at the University of Michigan, the University of Chicago, and the University of Virginia. Among his many distinguished books are *Dublin's Joyce*; *The Invisible Poet, T. S. Eliot*; *Samuel Beckett*; *The Stoic Comedians*; *The Pound Era*; *Bucky: A Guided Tour of Buckminster Fuller*; and *A Homemade World*.

ILSE DUSOIR LIND, professor of English at New York University, has held Ford Foundation and American Philosophical Society fellowships and has been Fulbright Lecturer in American Literature in Oslo, Norway, and visiting professor at the University of Hawaii. She has presented numerous papers and published several articles on Faulkner's works, including "The Teachable Faulkner," "The Design and Meaning of *Absalom, Absalom!*," and "Faulkner and Racism." In addition, she has for many years chaired the Special Faulkner Session at the national convention of the Modern Language Association.

THOMAS DANIEL YOUNG is general editor of bibliographies on Robert Penn Warren, Allen Tate, and Edmund Wilson; author

198

of numerous essays and reviews in such journals as *American Literature, Modern Fiction Studies,* and *South Atlantic Quarterly;* and coeditor, with R. C. Beatty and F. C. Watkins, of *The Literature of the South,* which has been a standard text in the field for more than a quarter of a century. Among the other works he has written or coedited are *American Literature: A Critical Survey; Donald Davidson: A Biographical and Critical Study;* and *Gentleman in a Dustcoat: A Biography of John Crowe Ransom.* Young is Gertrude C. Vanderbilt Professor of English at Vanderbilt University.